MEMORIES OF
the
CURRITUCK OUTER BANKS

AS TOLD BY ERNIE BOWDEN

CLARK TWIDDY

THE
History
PRESS

Published by The History Press
Charleston, SC
www.historypress.com

First published 2021

Manufactured in the United States

ISBN 9781467149471

Library of Congress Control Number: 2021937208

CONTENTS

AUTHOR'S NOTE

We have a responsibility to situate all of our work in a historical context so we can realize that history isn't this thing of the past, but it's something that we experience now.
—Corey Winchester, Evanston Township High School history teacher

O ver the time this book was written, we've seen a global pandemic reach even the shores of the distant Currituck Outer Banks. During the height of the pandemic, the sole bridge linking the world to the beaches was closed to visitors, and after the bridge reopening nearly eight weeks later, the Outer Banks as a whole has seen new levels of interest and popularity at a national level. This breathless recognition carries with it the winds of welcome commerce as well as the wistful knowledge that, as always, things will simply not be the same for the place or its people moving forward.

It is this wistful knowledge that provides much welcome context to these memories of a time seemingly incongruent and alien to the place we see today, and yet with a keen eye for history, the place today is revealed simply as the highwayed reflection of the salty cart paths and isolated surf men of an earlier time.

In seeking to understand the place fully, the mind's eye moves toward not what the place is or can be but rather whence it came and how. And no one alive today knows that story better than Ernie Bowden, of the Currituck Bowdens, one of the few remaining memory riders of a people who, long before the bridges were open, carved out a salted heritage in the fragile palm of the natural world. Lest we forget.

PREFACE

Institutionally, while the history of the United States Coast Guard is a worthy subject well documented in many other places, for our purposes here, it will be treated as simply the Coast Guard, although, in reality, it has taken several forms during the time in question. Today's Coast Guard, of course, is the inheritor of the traditions of the Revenue Cutter Service, the Lighthouse Service and, notably in our case, the United States Life-Saving Service that so defined the Outer Banks in the earliest creations of local Life-Saving Stations. Even today, the Coast Guard remains a key element of the Outer Banks fabric, with local surfboat stations and the nearby Elizabeth City Air Station—the largest of its kind in the world. To understand many of the beginnings of the Outer Banks we know today, look no further than the earliest Life-Saving Stations that become the anchor holds to Outer Banks families.

Geographically, Currituck County, the most northeastern county in the state and immediately adjacent to the Hampton Roads area of Virginia, is relatively unique in the state in that it has both an Outer Banks (beach) component and also a larger (in both size and population) mainland component. For the purposes of this work, the Currituck Outer Banks are considered the area of the Outer Banks from what is today just north of the Sanderling Resort in Duck to the Virginia Line. Currituck County is one of the oldest counties in the state and has many well-documented histories as well.

Lastly, in sharing this oral history Ernie's comments are combined with the author's contexts; to highlight the difference between the two, words in italics are used to share context while roman type is used for Ernie's language.

INTRODUCTION

A pilgrim's script—one man's field-notes of a land not far but unknown—
useful as that man loved the country he passed through and its folk, and
except as he willed to tell the truth. How other, alas, than telling it!
—William A. Percy, Lanterns on the Levee

Long before the Outer Banks became a nationally famous vacation
destination, this fragile group of gossamer islands along North
Carolina's northern coast was formed through an ancient and
elemental collision of nature. In the islands' invention, it was as if the
creator's giant hands simply clapped forth the flour dust that became the
very islands themselves. Rough Atlantic waters, charted by none other than
Ben Franklin himself, driven by relentless winds, clashed with mainland
rivers and sandy soils that would, in their meeting, sculpt some of the most
pristine and unique natural environments anywhere in the world. While
much has changed along these shores, these elemental collisions are still very
much in the identities of both those who live on the beaches and those who
love the beaches.

Notable as a place even from our earliest histories as a continent, the
Outer Banks has seen the early Native Indian tribes depart without a trace,
watched the arrival of mysterious Europeans seeking to carve out new
opportunities, been invaded multiple times as a result of its location, hosted
the brothers from Ohio as they sought powered flight and played roles in
both World War I and World War II as still more European visitors sought

to impose their will along these narrow shores. Beyond even these tectonic facets of history, nationally, the Outer Banks has for centuries also been known as a world-class fish and wildlife habitat. It is in that story we see many of the earliest intersections of development, commerce and visitation along these shores that, while less globally impactful, have become perhaps more locally defining in what the place itself has today become.

In a place rightly known for its visitors, at the same time, small families of native Outer Bankers have, through the generations, clung fiercely in their relative isolation to an independent and shared heritage intertwined with nature's movements—both loved and feared—on these shores. Over time, these small families evolved to represent a unique American group—isolated, slow to change, independent, self-reliant and, despite the pace of visitors, still even tribal in their ideas and identities. Few things unite people more than shared adversity, and the frequent storms that lashed these shores brought together a common mindset of self-reliance that marks Outer Bankers to this very day. Their generational voyage as a people is neither an exodus nor an arrival but a rooted embrace of nature and neighbor despite the winds of change.

The Bowden family is one of those rooted ocean tribes. The Currituck Outer Banks are their ancestral lands, and the salted firmament of this still-remote place retains their imprints long after the ceaseless wind has swept aside their sugar-sand footprints.

In sharing his oral memories, Mr. Ernie Bowden, at more than ninety years young, casts his remarkable memory from the storm-tossed isolation before the Wright Brothers to the very edge of the booming tourism industry of the twenty-first century. His journey recalls both things long forgotten—even disappeared—and things still defining in our sense of the place. In his memory, we come to know how this place came to be what it is today and the choices made in deciding, in many cases long ago, what it would in turn not be. From the small Coast Guard villages dotting the wind-whitened dunes in the early twentieth century to the commercial development of the modernized vacation mecca of the Currituck Outer Banks, Mr. Bowden's story combines the journey of small groups of defiant people in a distant place with the modern march of larger development in the face of an ongoing natural battle of sand, wind and water.

Before we begin to trace Mr. Bowden's footprints in the place, however, it's good to understand in advance a bit about the man making them. Ernie Bowden—referred to from here on as a respectful Mr. Ernie—was

Currituck Lighthouse, circa 1893. *Photo courtesy of the United States Coast Guard Historian's Office, with thanks to the Outer Banks Conservationists.*

born on the Outer Banks just north of what is now Corolla in 1925, just a few years after the First World War had concluded and during the presidency of Silent Calvin Coolidge. A fifth-generation native Outer Banker, he was and is, like many Outer Bankers, a doer of all things and as self-reliant as the endless summer day is long. He has been, at one time, a sailor, engineer, builder, farmer, horse trader, salvage specialist, an unwilling guest of the federal government, elected leader, livestock baron and, in some cases, all of those on the same day. Well into his eighties, Ernie Bowden was a daily and unchanging fixture light along the ever-growing crowds of suddenly here beachgoers, doing what he had always done—watching the waves, working the land, carving a life and trying to help his neighbors along the way.

It is elemental to note that this remote area—the far northeastern corner of North Carolina—orients both in people and in commerce to southeastern Virginia more so than any other place in North Carolina. In addition to the terrain, in understanding our story there remains one other tapestry at work: The Coast Guardsmen—and since time immemorial the families that follow them—make up a defining presence in his early life and those of his family.

The foundations for this book are, of course, Ernie's memories of the place. In sharing them formally, Mr. Bowden sat down with Michael E.C. Gary in the year 2010, and this book is a direct reflection of those recorded memories. In the scope of his memories, we move from the local birth of his grandparents just after the Civil War to his father, born in the same year as the famous first flight just south of Corolla, to a time where, far from forgotten, the Currituck Outer Banks now occupy a place of national prominence in the minds of residents and countless visitors alike. Like a great river, Ernie's memories tell the story of a place both changed and unchanged. In writing them, my intention is simply to understand, recognize and not forget what may to the eyes have disappeared over time.

FAMILY ROOTS

Like so many American families prior to World War II, the family world of the Bowdens was a local one, reflective of the horseback transportation horizons of the day—Ernie's family all hail from what we would today call simply the Outer Banks. While much of this horizon would be emblematic of other places—the mountains of Tennessee, for example, or the Mississippi Delta—what makes this horizon unique remains the sheer isolation of the place even with the arrival of early vehicles. These were self-reliant and capable people entirely at ease with existence on sand and water and very little else.

The villages that are described here are relatively close to each other and yet, to the modern seeker, are lost to the eye due to storms, the ever-moving fluid dynamics of windblown sand or even the developer's change-heralding bulldozer. The maps are the best guide to the place not as it is but as it was in Mr. Ernie's memory. The maps are our guide to the memories.

In addition, all through this book, it is impossible to underestimate the importance of the Coast Guard on the communities and families of the early Outer Banks; in most instances, the Coast Guard Station itself was the very centerpiece of the community and defined, in many respects, the heritage of the area. To understand the Bowden family is to also understand, in some small way, the birth and growth of the larger Coast Guard as an institution.

GRANDPARENTS FROM ALL SIDES

Both of my grandfathers were from Currituck County. My maternal grandfather was assigned to the Currituck Beach Coast Guard Station—his name was Lewis Lewark—while both of my grandmothers were from Nags Head. My paternal grandmother was Margaret Beasley. She left Nags Head when she was ten years old. Her mother had passed away and her father brought her to Knotts Island to live with an aunt; she met my grandfather there, and they were married on Knotts Island. She was a few years older than my maternal grandmother, and despite both being from Nags Head, they never knew each other when they lived in Nags Head.

My maternal grandmother was Eva Tillett, and she also hailed, as mentioned, from Nags Head. She met her husband, my grandfather Lewis Lewark, when he was transferred from the Currituck Beach Station to the Nags Head Station. My grandfather Lewark also served at one time in the Coast Guard at the Penny's Hill Station. He died in 1933 while he was stationed at the Currituck Beach Station. He did not die in the storm of that year; he was bedridden and died from a terminal illness just before the storm in the fall.

My paternal grandfather was William David Bowden. He was a commercial fisherman and a commercial market hunter who hunted ducks for the market. He became a duck hunter guide and then was in the commercial fishing industry. He died at the height of the Great Depression on December 29, 1929, as a result of a vehicle accident. He was transporting a catch of fish to a market in Norfolk and was in an accident on Virginia Beach Boulevard and died as a result of that accident. I didn't know my grandfather that well.

I was born on January 11, 1925, in my paternal grandmother's house in the Seagull community. She was a registered midwife, and she delivered children from Nags Head to Virginia Beach. She also had another house by that time up near the old Currituck Inlet near the original site of the Penny's Hill Coast Guard Station. That's where she lived in her later years. [It was in this home that she would die during the Ash Wednesday storm; Ernie touches on that later in the book.] My paternal grandmother left Seagull after my grandfather was killed in 1929, so we were in that house for only four years. Then she bought another house up in the community of Penny's Hill Coast Guard Station, which was just on the other side of the inlet. My grandmother was there until 1933, and the hurricane of 1933 destroyed that house also. Then she bought another house, which was in the same general area but was not damaged by the hurricane. It was a house that belonged to the officer in charge of the Penny's Hill Coast Guard Station who had retired.

My grandfather William Bowden was born in 1868, and my grandmother Margaret was born in 1878. She came here when she was ten years old, so that was 1888. She told me many times that her father brought her up this beach in a horse and wagon from Nags Head to live with her aunt and grow up over at Knotts Island because he didn't feel capable of raising her. When they came to the Currituck Inlet, we know today in Swan Beach, she said they had to wait for the tide to go out before they could get across that inlet with a horse and wagon in 1888. There was no ship traffic, but when the tide would go out, you could get across that inlet with a horse and wagon.

My grandfather built the house where I was born. My grandfather still owned the property at that time. A Mr. Neely Smith bought two and a half acres around the home, but my grandmother and grandfather continued to live there, although the home burned. I left there soon after I was born because my father was in the Coast Guard and he was transferred.

But my grandfather and grandmother left there in about 1928, because when the 1933 hurricane came, they were living in the Currituck Inlet area. They had relocated up there. My mother's family lived up in Seagull. She was going to school, and my grandfather, her father, was stationed at the Penny's Hill Coast Guard Station. He was transferred to the Currituck Beach Coast Guard Station, and they moved to Corolla and owned a house out there near the Coast Guard station.

The practice in those days was that a Coast Guardsman was stationed at Currituck Beach, and he had replaced someone else who was transferred to another station, and he purchased this man's house from him, who had been transferred elsewhere. He would be transferred from here to Hatteras or the Eastern Shore of Virginia or into Virginia Beach somewhere and he would be replaced, as my grandfather replaced some person, and he would purchase that person's house. It was a two-story house, and my mother had not completed the seventh grade up there when he was transferred to Corolla. There was this little one-room school there of course. She went to school there one year.

My mother and father both went to school in Swan Beach. I don't know if the school even had a name. It was moved in later years up to the Penny's Hill Coast Guard Station, and my grandmother purchased it and lived there following the 1933 hurricane. There used to be two churches right there at

Drawing of the Kill Devil Hills Life Saving Station. *Photo courtesy of Twiddy & Company.*

the head of Newfoundland Creek, a Methodist church and a Baptist church. The Methodist church was known as the Old Inlet Methodist Church. That school was right next to the property Doug Twiddy acquired from me a number of years ago. That school taught children through the seventh grade. The building, after, they didn't have any need for it anymore.

THE COROLLA LEWARK FAMILY

My grandfather Lewis Lewark was not related to the other Lewarks in Corolla village. If he was, I can't find any evidence of it. The patriarch of the Lewarks in Corolla was Mr. Tillman Lewark. He had a son Cleveland who was the caretaker for Mr. Knight at the Whalehead Club for all the years that the Knights owned it that I recall.

The other Lewark family was the John Lewark family, who owned that property that is known as Lewark Hill, but people call it Penny's Hill today, but it is really Lewark Hill. Old man John Lewark owned some ninety acres

Modern-day photo of the Whalehead Club.
Photo courtesy of Twiddy & Company.

there. It didn't go all the way to the mean high-water mark; it was kind of landlocked, but it was shaped sort of like a parallelogram.

He had a son named Will Lewark who was in the Coast Guard and was officer in charge of the Kill Devil Hills station until my father replaced him there. He had another son named St. Clair Lewark who was a federal game protector. Another son was Humphrey Lewark who lived in the village. Billy Griggs was old man "Hump" Lewark's great-grandson.

Billy Griggs's grandmother was named Odessa. She married a man named Griggs from over on the mainland. Captain Hump Lewark had three children. Captain Lewark died on his horse over on those dunes they called the Three Sisters. It was after he had retired from the Coast Guard. He had a herd of cattle, and he was out tending his cattle on his horse one day, and the horse came home without him. I remember that night I was at my grandmother's in the village, and all the neighbors who had vehicles with headlights went up on the dunes and shined their lights all around because they knew that was where his cattle were. But they didn't find his body that night. They found it the next day after daylight.

The John Lewark house is still under Lewark Hill. If you ever have an opportunity to see the December 1962 issue of *National Geographic*, it gives a very lengthy and definitive documentary on the Ash Wednesday Storm, which occurred in March of that year. There is a picture of the Lewark Hill and a group of people standing there at the second story of the John Lewark house peering in an open window.

FATHER AND MOTHER

My father's name was William Bowden, although everyone called him Captain Bill. He was born here on the Currituck Outer Banks. I'm the fifth generation of my family born right here. Dad was born November 9, 1903 [a little under a month before the Wright Brothers' famous flight]. My dad died in 1987, two days from being eighty-four. He died on the seventh of

November, and his birthday was on the ninth. My mother, Edith Lewark Bowden, died in 1999. She was ninety-two. Dad grew up here and didn't leave until he went into the Coast Guard.

He was nineteen when he married my mother. In 1923, my father entered the Coast Guard, and it was at that time we left the Seagull area and lived just to the north at the False Cape Coast Guard Station. My mother and father lived separate from my grandparents. Dad was there from 1923 to 1937 periodically. He would be away on various other missions. In 1927, Dad was in Florida with a group of Coast Guardsmen intercepting rumrunners coming in from Bermuda and the Bahamas during Prohibition. He was transferred from that duty to the same type of operation at Fire Island on Long Island in New York, where contraband whiskey was coming in.

In 1935, he was assigned to a relief group. The Coast Guard conducted relief and salvage operations in the Midwest as a result of the floods on the Mississippi and Missouri Rivers that year. The Coast Guard moved out there with their boats from the various stations; they were transported out there by rail, and they rescued people who were still stranded and houses that were surrounded by floodwaters. He was there for three months. Then he was on several other details. We didn't follow him to Florida, and we didn't follow him to New York at that time.

We stayed at the False Cape Coast Guard Station where we owned a home at that time. I was in school in Virginia. My dad served at the Wash Woods Station from July 1937 until September—just a very short time. Then he was transferred to Little Creek. Just before the war, he was assigned to a group charged with monitoring the movement of all Italian and German ships coming into the Hampton Roads port, and they would meet those ships at the twelve-mile limit, which we recognized as federal control limit; now it is two hundred miles, but back in those days, it was the twelve-mile limit we enforced under the federal laws in the United States. They met those ships there and towed them to their destination, whether it be a port in Norfolk or a port in Newport News or a port in Philadelphia or one in Baltimore.

This had everything to do with the war. Hitler had begun his campaign of world suppression in 1939 when he moved into Austria and Czechoslovakia, Poland and those countries. And, of course, England was right on the edge of everything. Most people didn't know at the time—and only those who have looked at history since then realize—that we were actively engaged in the war through England at the time. We gave England destroyers at one time before we ever became a part of the war. The Coast Guard had gotten some intelligence that some of these ships would be scuttled to block the harbors where large naval installations existed, such as Norfolk, Florida ports and Baltimore ports. They were very militarized, so that was really the reason for the Coast Guard arriving. That all changed with Pearl Harbor on December 7, 1941.

Dad had been on that assignment for about four months. Then at the beginning of the war, he was elevated to the rank of warrant officer. He was transferred to New York at the Manhattan Beach Coast Guard Station. That was a function that the Coast Guard had already started. They had several training stations set up, and that was one of them. My dad was assigned there, training men how to row boats and how to sail them—the boats that the Coast Guard used. Dad's next rank was lieutenant JG, then full lieutenant. Then he was transferred to the Pacific in late 1943. He was assigned to a service for the army. He was flotilla commander of a group of freight and supply ships that the Coast Guard manned for the army in their campaign of retaking of the Pacific Islands. They operated from immediately behind the landing forces. All these ships were refrigerated with freezer compartments. They loaded them with supplies and took the supplies up to those islands as they were being retaken. He came home at the end of the war and was assigned as the officer in charge of a Coast Guard cutter out of Virginia. He retired in 1947 as lieutenant commander.

I had two uncles who served in the Coast Guard. Roy Lewark was my mother's brother and David Bowden was my father's brother. They both

Wash Woods Station. *Photo courtesy of Doug Twiddy.*

served at the Wash Woods Station. My dad served there from July 1937 until September. Just a very short time. The Coast Guard had a rule that no two family members could serve at the same Coast Guard station. At that time, my mother's brother, Roy Lewark, was stationed there, and my dad was stationed there for just those several months. Then Dad was transferred to Little Creek in Virginia Beach.

My father was my mentor and certainly a person that I emulated. I thought he had done for himself things that not many people had accomplished from very meager beginnings. I have always respected my father for that. When I was in school in New York and he was still a boat officer there, we studied celestial navigation together. My father was a very accomplished navigator. He navigated that fleet of boats from Sturgeon Bay, Wisconsin, down the Mississippi River to the Gulf, through the Panama Canal up to Long Beach, California, and all the way across the Pacific and back and forth to Australia. He gained that ability through his own initiative. We studied something known as the Bowditch celestial navigation publication.

SCHOOL YEARS

I started school when I was only five years old. I lived with an aunt and uncle up in the Virginia Beach area and attended first grade. Then the next year the commanding officer at the False Cape Coast Guard Station had two sons who were school age. His wife transported them daily from False Cape to the Virginia Beach school, and I rode with them that year.

Then the old Princess Anne County in Virginia Beach allotted in their budget to fund a school bus to travel that portion of the beach from what was known in Virginia as the Wash Woods community, which was a small community on the state line, like Seagull and Corolla. A small group of people earned their livelihood from the area as fishermen or livestock owners—or in some cases Coast Guardsmen.

What industry existed there on the beach in those days was the livestock industry, commercial hunting and fishing and the Coast Guard. That school bus operated until 1937. The Coast Guard station at Wash Woods was decommissioned, as were a number of other Coast Guard stations on the coast. My dad was then transferred to Little Creek Coast Guard Station up in Virginia, and we moved up there. I completed my high school education at the same school where I began first grade.

My graduation from Oceana High School coincided with the beginning of World War II. I graduated from high school in June 1942, and we followed my father to New York, where he had been transferred as a boat officer at the Coast Guard training station. I entered prep school there to gain credits in trigonometry and advanced algebra that would allow me to enter an engineering school. I went to Boro Hall Academy in New York and the nearby Brooklyn Technical Institute. I also attended one year of engineering school at the Pratt Institute. During the war, I worked nights after school for the Sperry Corporation as a precision inspector inspecting bombsights and ninety-millimeter gunsights; I guess they thought that was more important than putting me in the military. We inspected parts for bombsights and gunsights that had tolerances of fifty-millionths of an inch. Those tolerances were measured with electric micrometers. Then my father was transferred to the Pacific, and our family moved back to the Tidewater area.

THE PLACES, STATIONS AND INLETS OF HOME

As the dunes of the Currituck Outer Banks shifted with the winds and waters, the dominant landmarks of the area remained the Coast Guard Stations themselves; not unlike the people, they were defiant in their ocean-facing fists of simple endurance. These stations were also the centers of people gravity over the years; schools, homes, boats and entire communities defined themselves by the station as much as anything else. Like the five boroughs of New York, the native Outer Bankers shared station identities as their common places and references.

THE SEAGULL COMMUNITY AND THE FIRST CURRITUCK INLET

The Seagull community was on the south side of the Currituck Inlet. The Penny's Hill Coast Guard Station and that little community was on the north side of the inlet. It was a little community oriented—as they all were—to the Coast Guard station. They lived right there near the station itself. There were probably forty or fifty families living here. They got back and forth to the mainland by boat out of the Currituck Inlet and from the village of Corolla. All of those folks who lived in the Seagull community were involved in the commercial fishing industry, hunting guides, commercial hunting and livestock industry. They used the practice of barter and trade between the people living here and the people living on the Currituck mainland. The

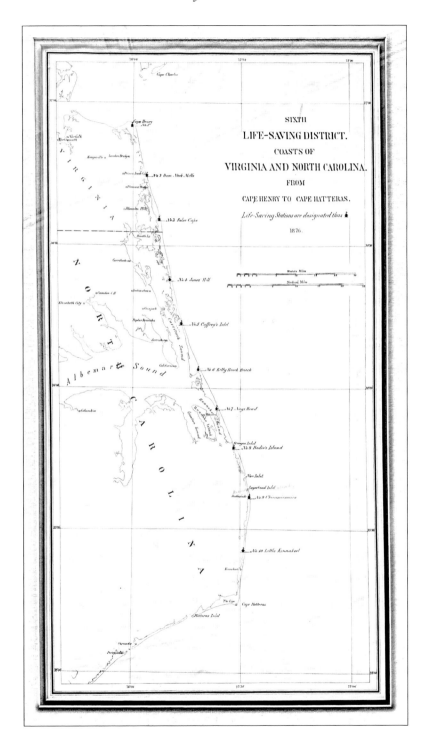

people here preserved fish with salt, known as a method of "corning" fish. The people from the mainland would come over here and trade things like corn from the farms over there to people here for corned fish. The people here had livestock and used the corn for feed.

The first Currituck Inlet was right at the site of the Virginia–North Carolina line. That is where there is a monument constructed of granite. It is my assumption that it almost had to be transported there by barge. And the inlet was certainly open at that time. There are several manuscripts and records of the actual surveys of its beginning, and it was terminated for a number of years, and they started to process it again, I think in 1803, and completed it that time. I never saw the inlet; it was closed up before I was born. I was born on January 11, 1925, in the community of Seagull.

THE CURRITUCK BEACH AND PENNY'S HILL COAST GUARD STATIONS

The Coast Guard, in many ways, was the very first developer of the Outer Banks. In their combined (recalling a combination of entities that merged into today's Coast Guard) efforts to save lives and safeguard commerce, the stations and lighthouses that the Coast Guard literally planted along the Outer Banks became the nucleus of today's towns and villages along the Outer Banks. The stations themselves, and the family communities around them, are inseparable from the history of not only the Outer Banks but also the families who populate them.

Along the Currituck Outer Banks, several prominent stations occupy key sites. Several of the original stations remain as examples of "town centers" of a long-ago Outer Banks. Notably, the family names of many of the surfmen in the stations remain prominent and locally rooted to this day.

For this memory, there are two key stations—Penny's Hill and the Currituck Beach Station—and each has been moved over time from its original location. The Penny's Hill Station burned, however, and one remains today in private hands.

While the back-and-forth movement can get confusing, here's the key—the Currituck Beach Station today stands on the site of the original Penny's Hill Station.

Kill Devil Hills Life Saving Station with surfmen. *Photo courtesy of Twiddy & Company.*

The actual Penny's Hill site was on the north side of the Currituck Inlet, and it disappeared over time due to the movement of sand and the impact of storms—remember, what we call Penny's Hill today was known in earlier times as Lewark's Hill. Today, around the old site of the southern inlet—where the first Penny's Hill Station was built—is the old Currituck Beach Coast Guard Station. That station's original location was on eight and a half acres of what is today the resort community of Corolla Light. There's a good story there, and it involves a lady named Lynn Lockhart and a famous Corolla developer named Richard "Dick" Brindley.

In short, Lynn bought both stations from Mr. Brindley, and they were both moved from the Corolla Light area to the site of the original Penny's Hill Station.

To get a sense of how all of this movement came to be, let's start with the Second World War, during which the Whalehead Club was essentially operated by the military. Right after World War II, Mr. Adams bought the Penny's Hill Station, in addition to the entire Whalehead Club itself. After Mr. Adams died and the property was sold, the Penny's Hill Coast Guard Station was sitting back there very close to the boathouse at Whalehead.

Wash Woods Station. *Photo courtesy of Doug Twiddy.*

Lynn Lockhart bought it from the developers and had it moved out to the nearby property where the Currituck Beach Station was located.

As the Corolla Light area developed as a resort, Mr. Dick Brindley approached Lynn Lockhart and negotiated a purchase of the property that Lynn owned there. To Lynn's credit, she wanted to keep those two Coast Guard stations, and I knew Mr. Brindley quite well. He called me once and asked me if I knew of any property for sale up this way. I told him that there was a two-and-a-half-acre parcel up around old Seagull that was for sale. So, Mr. Brindley bought it and had those two Coast Guard stations moved north at the same time.

In the end, the Penny's Hill Coast Guard Station came back to within a few hundred feet of where it was constructed right after the Civil War. Unfortunately, that station caught fire and burned, but the Currituck Beach Coast Guard Station is located on the site of the original Penny's Hill Station; it's still in private Lockhart hands.

THE WASH WOODS COAST GUARD STATION

The Wash Woods Coast Guard Station, in addition to the Penny's Hill Station and the Currituck Beach Station, was one of three Coast Guard Stations in the area over time. Built in 1917, the station is fully restored today and is in private hands, although it is open to the public. It is one of the few remaining examples of an early twentieth-century operating Coast Guard station. After World War II, many of the last remaining stations closed in part due to the advancements of technology that made manned beach patrols, in watching the ocean, less effective than air patrols out of nearby Elizabeth City.

In 1952, I was operating a hunt club in what was for many years the Wash Woods Coast Guard Station that had been built in 1917, partly as a result of World War I. I had bought that 550 acres of land at what is today part of Section 10 of Carova Beach. I was operating a duck hunting club using the Wash Woods Coast Guard Station as a clubhouse. We leased the Coast Guard station. My dad was a close friend of Admiral Wood, who was commander of the Fifth Coast Guard District. The Coast Guard was not selling the station or getting rid of it altogether; they were going to put it in a caretaker status. My dad talked to them. They had one guy stationed there at the time; one Coast Guardsman and his wife lived at the station. A boy by the name of Midgett and my dad talked to Admiral Wood, and he agreed to lease it to us. We leased it for twenty years, from 1952 to 1972. I operated a duck hunt club there all that time in conjunction with the livestock business I was doing

Kabler and Riggs Realty office. *Photo courtesy of Larry Riggs.*

and whatever construction I was doing in the meantime in the Carova Beach subdivision. That hunt club entertained members of the professional community, doctors and attorneys and people of that nature who were interested in a membership in a private duck club. We just called it the Bowden Club.

We had it before Kabler and Riggs got it. They got it in 1970. Sam Riggs asked me if I would burn it. I knew Pat Crowder in Richmond, and I knew she was looking for a Coast Guard station, so she came down and bought it and the two oceanfront lots in front of it. Then I renovated that building. They wanted central heat, so I put in electric baseboard heat, carpet and had all the windows rebuilt. There was a place in Virginia Beach, a mill supply house, that rebuilt all the original windows. I also put the plumbing in it. Prior to that, the plumbing was very meager. I put a septic tank in and replaced all the plumbing. I also added a new roof—the old roof had been a slate roof, but it had been damaged by lightning strikes several times over the years.

SEAGULL COMMUNITY CEMETERY

There are only two cemeteries on the Currituck Outer Banks that I know of. One is the old Neely Smith cemetery. There is only one headstone with a name on it: Mr. Neely Smith's son. There is another stone with a name on it—H.L. Smith. That was Hub Smith, a commercial fisherman who drowned while fishing in March—born October 5, 1883, drowned March 15, 1912. Commercial fishermen back in those days wore hip boots; today, a lot of the commercial fishermen wear waders that are armpit length. Supposedly, the boy Hub Smith had a new pair of hip boots, and the fishing dory they were using to set nets turned over. The first rule when you were fishing in the ocean and got in trouble was to kick your hip boots off. Hub refused to get rid of his boots because they were brand new, and in effect, it cost him his life. The other people in the boat with him swam to shore. But Hub drowned because his boots filled with water. Everybody always bought boots about a size too large so you could get them off.

His father was G.F. Smith, who is buried there—January 30, 1856, died May 19, 1920. Mr. Neely Smith's wife, Ms. Love Smith, was a sister to Mr. Leon White, who owned the 480 acres in the area that is still owned by his heirs. The last count I think there were over four hundred heirs, and they have gotten signatures from all of them, except one heir who lives in Australia. They haven't been able to get his signature for a purchase. Mr. Neely Smith lived up on the Currituck Inlet with Ms. Love Smith's sister in the same area. There were several houses up there. The post office address was known as Seagull back in those days. The settlement was right on the bank of the Currituck Inlet. People decorated the gravesites with conch shells. Some people didn't even have a headstone. I'm sure some of the small children didn't have a headstone. You'll find a block of cement marking the grave, and I guess in some cases, you'll find a conch shell marking a gravesite. I don't know any other people who were buried there except Mr. Neely Smith and Hub. The headstones are in good shape.

Swan Beach Churches

There were two churches in Swan Beach, right there close to the school, and there is a cemetery there, right at the head of Newfoundland Creek, right next to the telephone company hut, they call it. That little building up there that is enclosed with an anchor fence, the telephone company refers to them as huts. They have transferring equipment inside—some technology they have developed where they do a lot of finger work. Right next to it there is a one-acre site that is a cemetery, and I think there is only one tombstone left in there—Mr. Caleb Barco. He was my maternal great-grandmother's second husband. His tombstone is the only one left there. Somebody vandalized all the others. There was an old shipwreck survivor, Neely somebody, a Scandinavian name, was shipwrecked and survived the wreck, made it to shore in that area and settled there in the Seagull community with some of the natives there, and his tombstone was in that cemetery.

My father had a brother, who would have been older than he, who died at birth and was buried in that cemetery. There were about fifteen tombstones in there when I was a child, but some out-of-town teenagers carried them away in the 1950s. The deputy sheriff in Corolla at that time was a native by the name of Griggs O'Neal—we all called him Barney Fife, a nickname—but it was his mother who died with my mother during the Ash Wednesday Storm. He was living here in Corolla at that time. This vehicle came by and stopped out there to get gasoline, and the deputy happened to be there. It was an open Jeep vehicle, and he noticed in the back seat there were all these tombstones. He approached the people and asked about the tombstones. They said they found them up on the beach, back in the woodland, and they were going to take them with them. He made them unload them. He lived in a house that was just inside the Whalehead complex on the left. If you go in from the lighthouse, drive down the neighborhood road and keep straight ahead, there used to be a house on the left that Mr. Ray Adams built as a residence for some of the employees he employed at the Whalehead Club. After the club was sold to

Mr. McLean—Mr. McLean owned all of Whalehead at one time—Griggs O'Neal lived there, along with his father. He lost his mother, as I said.

Anyway, he had those fellows unload those tombstones right beside the steps at the entrance of that house. I saw them there several times in visiting Griggs there. They left Mr. Caleb Barco's stone that is still there. They drove on down the beach to Corolla, and at that time, the deputy sheriff was Griggs O'Neal. They stopped down there at Mr. Johnny Austin's store. Mr. Johnny used to sell Coca-Colas and candy bars in that tiny place he had there. They stopped to get a Coca-Cola or something, and the deputy noticed the tombstones in the back of that Jeep. They were cooperative; they just told him they found the cemetery and took the stones. He took the stones.

Griggs took those stones back to his house and placed them right beside the steps going into his house. I saw them there many times myself. Later on, as Corolla grew, the Whalehead Club got developed by this group out of New Jersey, and they tore that house down and tore down another house that was there.

Lynn Lockhart moved the old Penny's Hill Coast Guard Station away from the Whalehead Club at the same time. I went to look for those old tombstones, and they were gone. At one point recently, I bumped into a telephone service, Rick Lumpkin from over on Spot Road. He told me that Griggs O'Neal gave him those stones to put back on one of his trips up here to service that telephone hut. He says he put them on the ground and covered them with a shovel right beside the remaining tombstone.

There is a cemetery up in the [Virginia] False Cape State Park. Fortunately, the Virginia Park Service has cleaned up a portion of that cemetery and built a picket fence around it. It's quite a popular place for folks visiting and walking that path. A friend of mine sent me a picture of the steeple part of the church when it was still standing. Why is just the steeple left? The old church fell down and there were some people living in the False Cape State Park at that time. Two young boys lived up there at the time named the Murphy brothers. The old steeple was still laying on the ground where it had fallen off the church. They took that steeple in a truck or something out to their residence out on the oceanfront in what is today the False Cape Park and set it up out there on a dune, and it stayed there for a number of years. The state was steadily buying up that property piece by piece as it came available. They came to that spot, and Mr. Harry Murphy was the person who actually owned that lot. He was the grandfather of these two teenagers. The state bought that property

Wash Woods Church located in False Cape State Park. *Photo courtesy of Larry Riggs.*

and then some of the state people took that steeple back over to the site of the church, and that's how it comes to be there today.

During the late 1950s, a veterinarian from the Virginia Beach area, Dr. Eddie Shorin, bought a little piece of property right near the church, just maybe a quarter of a mile to the south. He and his wife took it upon themselves to try to restore that church. They collected donations from various individuals and I suppose a few businesspeople in Virginia Beach. They started a little project of restoration, and it never got off the ground. Their intent was good.

THE VERY FIRST NORTH CAROLINA STATE LINE

The granite monument up there is the actual beginning of the State of North Carolina. Every schoolchild in North Carolina should visit it. The Virginia Institute of Marine Science did an article on the survey that began the separation of the portion of land that eventually became North Carolina from Virginia. It gives us an eyewitness account of one portion of the survey. It went on for years before it was ever completed.

Some political factors got involved in the thing, as usual. Somewhere up in Danville, Virginia, there was a farmer with political clout, and the survey was going to cut his farm in half, and he was well enough established that he could stop the survey. It took them several years to reroute the survey. If you ever look close at a state map of the Virginia–North Carolina state line, you will find that little jog in it where it bypassed his farm.

The U.S. Fish and Wildlife now owns this property where the monument is, but I asked the developers to set aside a twenty-foot public easement and a one-hundred-foot right-of-way back to the monument. I have hoped to get an elevated walkway, something eighteen to twenty-four inches above the ground, that would allow people to visit that thing. The county put a fence around it to keep the ATV riders from driving all over it.

THE OPEN BOUNDARY OF VIRGINIA AND NORTH CAROLINA

When I was a child, all that area at the state line was open—not wooded at all because cattle grazed there. We were still experiencing over wash from the ocean in the spring and in the fall, which prevented the growth of vegetation. I thought for many years that the monument was marble, but it isn't. It's granite. I came here one time with a black Magic Marker and traced all those things so they would show up; originally, they were the same color as the nine granite, and you could hardly read them. It was just something I thought was necessary. On it is the only abbreviation of North Carolina that I have ever seen like it: "N.Ca."

The old Currituck Inlet was up there. They have determined that the inlet when it was open was about 1,200 feet wide. I have to believe that the monument came in on a barge. With that kind of granite weight, it had to have come right in the inlet and set up in 1887. The original survey took place in 1728, but that is when they started. The eyewitness accounts that I have read say that they drove a cedar post there. They rerouted the survey, but they finished it, and when they resurveyed this thing in 1887, some forty years later, they found it was only off approximately 3 feet from the original survey.

When I was a child, we used to herd cattle and sheep right there, and there was a big dipping vat down in the woods. It was on the Linwood Dudley tract, corrals and all. That was where we would corral the cattle and run them through that dipping vat. So, the inlet was said to be 1,200 feet wide. The accounts I have read said the groups were camped on the north side of the inlet, and one account says some of these guys had their wives with them. They were living in tents, the commissioners and surveyors and all. One account says that they looked across the inlet one morning and there was a recluse, or some other name they called it, gathering mollusks, clams or something from the ocean, and he was accompanied by a harlot with no clothes on and hair down past her waist. That was on the Carolina side of the inlet. We didn't make any distinction back in those days between this imaginary state line. People from there visited here, and people from here visited there. Even people from one community married the other. My grandfather had a sister who married Burr Ewell, who lived in Virginia. I don't know how many marriages like that took place. Mr. Burr Ewell, who lived in the Wash Woods community, married my great-aunt, who lived in Carova Beach. A man by the name of Timothy Bowden, one of my forebears, owned a strip of land from Currituck Sound to the ocean, and his neighbor owned an adjoining strip, the same thing. Both had 170 acres in each strip. That was the property where my grandfather was born and my great-grandfather.

The old Wash Woods village's primary claim to fame up there is that it was always the first voting precinct in the state of Virginia to record its vote, because in its heyday there may have been twenty people to vote up there. I remember when I was about six or seven years old, the candidate for clerk of court in old Princess Anne County, Virginia, came down the beach to campaign in the Wash Woods precinct. My dad was stationed at the False Cape Station, and he took me with him to go down there. There was a little old one-room school there, like the one in Corolla. My dad took me with him to meet the candidate. The candidate that year was named William Frank Hudgins. All the people on the beach back in those days were small in stature. Hardly anybody was taller than I am now. Captain Roy Dudley was about the tallest person I knew on this beach, and maybe Mr. Pell Austin, who

Modern photo of the Corolla Schoolhouse. *Photo courtesy of Twiddy & Company.*

was taller than his brother Johnny. We went down there and walked in that school. We were there a little early. Pretty soon, the candidates came—Sidney Gallop and W.F. Hudgins. Mr. Hudgins stood about six foot eight inches tall. When I saw that man, I didn't think there was anybody in the world as big as that guy. I can remember it like it was yesterday.

THE DUDLEY FAMILY AND DUDLEY'S ISLAND

I've always had respect for older people, and one sticks out other than my dad—Captain Roy V. Dudley. He was my father's first officer in charge at the False Cape Coast Guard Station, and he also traveled with my Dad to Florida on those rumrunning things and to Fire Island Inlet and out to the Midwest. Mr. Dudley and my father were not only shipmates—and he was my dad's commanding officer at the surf station—but they also developed a very close relationship. They stayed in touch until Mr. Dudley died first. After his death, of course, that friendship ended, but we still stayed in touch with Mrs. Dudley until she passed away.

Mr. Dudley was a person that I certainly had a great deal of respect for, and I felt that he had some influences over things I thought about and things I did later on. It sounds a little homey, I suppose, but many times when I'd be doing something I would think to myself, "Would my dad approve of this?" or "would Mr. Dudley be proud of whatever I'm doing?"

Mr. Dudley's uncle was the real famous decoy carver Lee Dudley. Lee Dudley was a twin to Mr. Dudley's father. They were Lee and Linwood. Lee Dudley owned a hunt club over what we call Munden's Point. It is actually in North Carolina—part of the Mackay Island Wildlife Refuge now—and that is where Mr. Lee Dudley is buried. Mr. Lee Dudley was never married and naturally didn't have any children. Mr. Linwood Dudley, however, had three children—Linwood, Roy and a daughter who married Joe Stevens from up in the Wash Woods community. They owned the Dudley Hunt Club in Virginia, which adjoins the Carova Beach property on the back up near the state line. Mr. Lee Dudley, Linwood Dudley and his father—his name was Linwood too—they started that hunt club that was only about a quarter of a mile from the Virginia–North Carolina line in Virginia. They owned what was known as Deal's Island—about four hundred acres in that piece of property. All of Deal's Island lay in North Carolina. Part of their property was in Virginia, but the majority of the hunt club property was in North Carolina in the form of Deal's Island.

That property on Deal's Island Creek was all owned by Mr. Linwood Dudley. Mr. Linwood Dudley was nephew to Lee Dudley, the world-renowned decoy duck carver. His decoys today, if you could find one, start at about $50,000 [and that was in 2010; they'd no doubt be worth more than that today.]

At one time, Roy Dudley wanted to trade me my five hundred acres of land right back of the Wash Woods Coast Guard Station. Roy Dudley was a Coast Guardsman and married old Captain Knight's daughter. He was the captain of the old original Wash Woods Coast Guard Station at one time.

Anyway, Mr. Lin Dudley operated that hunt club. Dudley's Island was a portion of marshland. We used to have terrible ice storms here in the winter. The bay would freeze and stay frozen for a month or month and a half at a time. When that ice would break up, it would tear down

Beachgrass on Currituck's Outer Banks. *Photo courtesy of Larry Riggs.*

all the duck blinds and cut off lots of marshes. In fact, in 1941, it destroyed the Currituck Sound bridge, and it was out for about thirty days before they got it repaired for vehicular traffic. I drove the first car across it from west to east. My dad was in charge of the Kill Devil Hills Coast Guard Station at that time, and he and I got to that bridge for him to go back on duty, and he had to walk across a walkway where the damaged part was being repaired, and a Coast Guard truck from the station came up there and picked him up, and I stayed there with the car until they got it repaired enough for one-way traffic later that afternoon.

I went on down to the Kill Devil Hills Station, where he was later that day. That ice in Back Bay supposedly cut a great big portion of marshland loose, and it was drifting down with the ice. The story went that Mr. Linwood Dudley's father, old man Linwood Dudley, this marsh chunk came close to his clubhouse, and he supposedly went out there with some stakes of some kind and stabilized it, and the marsh continued to grow in real shallow water and grounded itself, and he laid claim to it. That's where Dudley's Island came from.

THE COROLLA VILLAGE, POST OFFICE AND WHALEHEAD CLUB

While the Currituck Outer Banks as a place came to be as a result of many individuals, few people have had as much cumulative impact as two: Joseph Palmer Knapp and Edward C. Knight. Their love of the area, first defined by their association with some of the finest private duck clubs in history, marks a departure point in the development of the Currituck Outer Banks.

J.P. Knapp was a national publisher and philanthropist; among his many wildlife conservation efforts was the founding of what is today Ducks Unlimited. A conservationist and lover of the Currituck Outer Banks, he also donated what is now the Mackay Island National Wildlife Refuge, and Currituck's Early College today bears his name. His impact on Currituck County, in seeking to balance development with nature, is difficult to measure.

Northern railroad executive Edward C. Knight was the builder of the simply opulent Whalehead Club. The club became a foundation for many things in the area, not least of which was some of the earliest residential development in Corolla. Today, the club itself is intact and operated by Currituck County.

Along the modern Outer Banks, the Corolla area today is the most developed community of the Currituck Outer Banks, with grocery stores, restaurants and all the facets of a resort community. It is visited by hundreds of thousands of tourists per year, and many of the old places are key attractions.

Mr. Knight's Whalehead Club remains a pristine example of the extravagance of some of the turn-of-the-century private duck clubs. It

Corolla Post Office. *Photo courtesy of Larry Riggs.*

has become, like some of the Coast Guard stations themselves, a defining presence in the area. It is not an accident that the club is almost literally in the shadow of the Currituck Beach Lighthouse, built in 1870, or that the village of Corolla sprang up around a combination of Coast Guard development and habitat tourism.

The old village today remains largely intact as it was in Mr. Ernie's memory. The old one-room schoolhouse still stands and is, happily, the smallest public school in the state. The other buildings have in part converted to small shops and stores but retain their architectural congruence with what is perhaps the best surviving example in the state of an old fishing village recalled in the time of Mr. Ernie's youth.

For many years, the post office, like so many other places, was the center of the community in many ways and offered, in an earlier time, one of the few places with news of the outside world.

When I was six or eight years old and I could first remember things, Mr. Sol Sanderlin was the postmaster in the Corolla village. He lived where Norris Austin has that little thing they call the Outback something or another, right there next to his apartment. But Sol Sanderlin's post office sat right there in his house. He was the postmaster, and he sold kerosene and gasoline out of fifty-gallon drums. They used to deliver it to the public dock right there where the fence used to go down to the water at the Whalehead Club. They would bring it over there in fifty-gallon drums and get it up on the dock. Mr. Sol Sanderlin, somehow or other, would get it over to his place. He had a metal can that looked like a metal milk can but shaped just a little bit different on top. Inside that thing there was a piece of metal soldered to the can itself, and the point of it was like an arrow point. Up to that arrow point measured exactly five gallons of gasoline.

He had an old boat pump he used to pump water out of a boat in those days. It was just a plain piece of pipe with a stick thing that went down inside of it, had a piece of leather on it that would expand. And you lifted it up and down and pumped the water out of the boat and overboard. He used it to pump gasoline out of that barrel and into that can to measure it.

Mr. Johnny Austin became postmaster after Mr. Sol retired, and he took over the same job—even took over the same building. He had to move it a little bit to get it on his property, a little old building. It had a little row of mailboxes on one side of it. I remember when I was a child, Mr. Sol had a glass-front candy case, and he kept candy in it. Every time I would get a nickel, dime or fifteen cents together, I would walk over there. My maternal grandmother and grandfather Lewark lived right close to where the Currituck Beach Coast Guard Station was in the village [this is one of the few mentioned homes still standing today]. My maternal grandfather was stationed there. I came down to stay with them sometimes, and my grandfather had a garden right across the road from the Corolla Lighthouse. He would give me some of the vegetables out of there to sell. Radishes and cucumbers were about all I got because he produced more of those than the family could use. There was a group of people that lived all around the Coast Guard Station, about ten or twelve houses. I would take some cucumbers out there and walk from house to house and sell them, two cucumbers for a nickel and a bunch of radishes for a nickel. I would sell those things out there, and when I would get ten or twenty cents, I would walk through that hot sand all the way up to Mr. Sol's post office to buy a candy bar out of that glass case.

When I was a child, there used to be a merry-go-round in the yard at the Whalehead Club. It was a galvanized pipe that reached about twelve or fourteen feet above the ground, and it had all these steel rods that came down in a hexagon shape. Those rods were attached to a galvanized angle iron frame, and the seats were bolted to those frames. The children would sit on those seats, and that thing rotated on a pin on top of that pole. Children would sit on the seats, and one or two would push it. That thing would go round and round and round. Some of those boys would get rambunctious and push that thing in toward the pole. One of the children lost the end of her finger when those boys pushed that thing up toward that pole. It struck the end of her finger and cut it off. I lost a tooth the same way when I was about eight or nine years old.

We learned as children growing up here how to entertain ourselves. Nail kegs, for example, years ago were wooden kegs. They were small at the bottom and small at the top and larger in the middle. They had round metal rings that held them together. The boys, if they could find an old metal ring off of a nail keg, we would take a heavy piece of straight wire, and you could make a fancy crook in the bottom of it. You could put that thing against that metal hoop and start pushing it. You would just hold that piece of wire on and run with the thing, and it would fly. That was one toy we made ourselves. We used to make our own slingshots. Take an old automobile inner tube, go in the woods and find an old persimmon tree that had a fork in it; whittle that thing out with an old Barlow knife. All the kids had Barlow knives; they cost fifty cents. With one blade in it, we'd whittle that thing out and use those rubber tire bands. And if you could find an old shoe with a leather tongue in it, you could cut a hole in it, tie that rubber band to it, tie it to those forks in the tree and use the leather part of it for whatever you had to shoot. Some of the boys became real proficient with that thing. They could shoot a bird with it.

Modern photo of the Whalehead Club. *Photo courtesy of Twiddy & Company.*

During that same time, the Whalehead Club had a big board fence around the entire compound area over there. It started down at the water and came up about where the lighthouse is, went a little farther, then turned and went south way down the shoreline and back out to the water. That was to prevent anybody who was not invited from getting in around the clubhouse. They had two gates. There was a gate right where the entrance is today to go back to today's Wildlife Education Center, and there was another gate about probably three hundred or four hundred feet from this corner going down that east fence where Mr. and Mrs. Knight [Edward Collings Knight Jr. and his wife, Marie Louise] would travel out through that gate over to the oceanfront.

Mr. Knight had given Mr. Knapp about seven or eight acres of land behind what is now the Currituck County offices. Mr. Knapp would visit, come over here by boat and he and the Knights would have elegant dinners at the clubhouse. I guess the main thing that attracted me to that building out there that Mr. Knapp built was that it was a very simple beach cottage–type house, but it had a huge fireplace in it—a great big brick fireplace—and we would sometimes pass by it and see it. That fireplace always fascinated me. Helen Lewark later got that piece of property and sold it to someone from Virginia. I think it was eight and a half acres of it. She developed it into that little residential subdivision right behind the county offices. That was the property Mr. Knapp owned. At the time, Mr. Cleveland Lewark was the caretaker for the Whalehead Club for Mr. Knight. And his wife, Mrs. Grace Lewark, taught school in Corolla. They lived in the caretaker's house, which was a little beyond that house I referred to that Griggs O'Neal lived in. I remember Mrs. Grace Lewark played and taught piano. My mother took piano lessons from Mrs. Grace Lewark. She taught her classes at the Corolla one-room schoolhouse.

EARLY MOTOR VEHICLES

My dad used to tell me he had a Model T Ford he got when he was nineteen years old, just before he and my mother were married. He told me that Mr. Ben Malbon, who was the officer in charge at the Penny's Hill Coast Guard Station, may have had one of the first motor vehicles here. You could drive a Model T on the beach. Those old things had 475 by 18s. The tire was only 4.75 inches wide, and the wheel was 18 inches in diameter. They used to say that when Captain Malbon would leave to go up to Virginia Beach on liberty, he, his wife and two sons—he had small children—they would get into that old Model T Ford and drive it over to the ocean and then would drive on low water all the way to Virginia Beach. The Coast Guard crew would push that thing. Captain Malbon kept it garaged in a little wooden garage he had behind the Coast Guard station and his house. It would take the whole crew to push it over to the ocean. The first vehicle I ever had was a Model A Ford. I was fourteen years old. You could get your driver's license when you were fourteen in those days. I got it from a guy and gave him two bicycles and twenty dollars for it.

STORIES OF A WORKING LIFE UPON A GLITTERING OCEAN

COMMERCIAL FISHING: FROM STURGEON TO CAVIAR ALONG THE SHORES

Now very much illegal to fish, sturgeon was once considered a delicacy and, as a result, a prized catch. Money from sturgeon fishing carried, as Mr. Ernie points out, many a family through the winter.

My grandfather W.D. Bowden was a commercial fisherman and lived in the old Seagull community. He and his fishing partner, Mr. John Whitson, were the last of the commercial fishermen who fished for sturgeon. That was a fish they primarily fished for, and they fished for them twelve miles out in the ocean. They rowed a dory out there, as they didn't have any motors in those days. Their object was to catch what's known as cow sturgeon, the female. A sturgeon doesn't spawn until it's twelve years old. These fish they would catch would probably weigh three hundred pounds; a cow sturgeon that they would save would be so large the two men couldn't get it in the boat, so they would lash it to the boat with ropes and tow it to shore by rowing that dory. It reminds me of *The Old Man and the Sea.* They would bring a horse and cart over to the beach and load that sturgeon and extract the roe.

Mr. John Whitson's wife—I don't know what her name was, we always called her Ms. Wid—and my grandmother, everybody called "Lady Bug," together, it was their job to process this roe into caviar. The process was to

Fishermen on Currituck's Outer Banks. *Photo courtesy of Larry Riggs.*

first salt it, like you would salt fish or salt hams. After it has been salted for a certain length of time, they would take the roe, which would be in two pieces, pretty large, and hang it on a clothesline and dry it in the sun. Then they would take it down and use a cheesecloth as a sieve and massage that roe by hand to separate the mucous that holds the eggs together from the eggs. The eggs would pass through the cheesecloth into a container underneath. Of course, it is all salted and dried and cured. Then they placed it in glass jars like fruit jars.

To get it to market, my grandfather or Mr. John would take it up to Munden's Point in Virginia and ship it by railroad from there to New York, where it would be sold at a great price. If they would catch a cow sturgeon in the spring, that would be enough cash to carry them until the fall. Then they would begin to depend on duck hunting.

THE IMPORTANCE AND DEVELOPMENT OF WATERFOWL HUNTING

While the first manned flight of the Wright brothers in Kill Devil Hills might be the region's chief contribution to history, it didn't at the time make an economic impact locally. For that, it's tough to underestimate the local impact of the 1918 conservation law prohibiting so-called market-hunting that changed many a way of life along the sounds and inlets. Nationally, the brisk market for birds and bird feathers was decimating bird populations around the world, and the story of the passage of the act is a great read relating to federal versus state law in itself. For our purposes, this law forbade the shooting of waterfowl for the purpose of selling it and, at one swoop, ended one way of life and created another—waterfowl guiding associated with the large private hunt clubs and a small but growing number of hunting-minded visitors. While still a relatively small number, the first forms of Outer Banks tourism were invariably focused not on the ocean but on the sounds as waterfowl habitat; look no further than many of the famous duck clubs of the age for the first examples of today's modern beach homes. Even to this day, none surpass the Whalehead Club in extravagance, and almost all the old clubs were built on the sound as opposed to the ocean.

In 1918, the federal government prohibited the hunting and sale of migratory waterfowl. That law prohibited the taking of swans, among many other things; we called them trumpeter swans. All throughout this whole area, the Albemarle and Currituck area of North Carolina, lots of people were water-oriented or worked on the water, and in times like Thanksgiving and Christmas, we always had a swan instead of a turkey.

My grandfather was the first person arrested and prosecuted for killing a swan after the government made it illegal. You have to understand that back in those days, this area was so remote, it had very little contact with other parts, even the Currituck County mainland area, so he was not aware of the law. He was a deeply religious person. My father and my neighbor and my grandfather fished together when my father was about fourteen years old. He did commercial fishing in the sound and on the oceanfront as well. My grandfather would not fish on Sunday; in fact, he wouldn't do anything at all on Sunday. He wouldn't even let my father and the neighbor leave the house until after midnight on Sunday night. Commercial fishermen fished a lot at night in the sound, particularly in the spring, when the fish were beginning to break up into smaller groups where they had been schooled up in large groups in deep water during the winter. In the spring, the water would warm up, and these fish would start to break up and move around in shallower water. A lot of

Seagulls on Currituck's Outer Banks.
Photo courtesy of Larry Riggs.

times the commercial fishermen would choose to fish at night. My dad and Elwood couldn't leave that house until after midnight, so he would not have shot that swan if he had known that it was illegal. He had shot that swan for Christmas dinner.

Hunting and Fishing Landings and Congregations

They didn't have any motors except for a few people who had the money to buy an inboard kind of motor. They called them "motor go's" and "make-n-brakes" back in those days; they were just simple air-cooled motors. Most people did what we called "shoving" a boat. Some people referred to it as "poling," using a shoving paddle. My grandfather had been out somewhere and killed that swan, had it laying right there in the boat, pure daylight and was poling the boat back into the landing. There was always a group of people around a public landing like that back in those days—always somebody mending a net or working on a boat, just folks congregating, mostly men. My grandfather shoved right up there to the wharf, tied his boat up, picked his swan up and started walking up the wharf. The game warden was standing right there at the dock—gave him that ticket, and they prosecuted him for it. The fine was $500, but I'm sure he didn't pay that much, cause I'm sure he didn't have $500 more than two or three times a year. That was what we called the old Station Landing, near the original Penny's Hill Station.

There was a little creek that branched off of the Currituck Inlet. The Currituck Inlet that we know, that is all filled in now but was opened for a short period by the Ash Wednesday Storm. That landing, everybody in the neighborhood used that landing or used the old inlet. Or if they were down near Lewark Hill, they used the landing there called Jack's Creek, right east of the Monkey Island Hunt Club.

People just maintained those docks themselves. It was a community effort. If a pole rotted off or broke off, somebody went there and put a new one in. If part of the deck got rotten, maybe several of the folks would get together, pick up some lumber off the beach and replace those boards that were getting broken or rotten. My grandfather never used a profane word, and in church, he led the choir. His favorite hymn was "The Old Rugged Cross." He was a deacon in that same church, the Currituck Inlet

Methodist Church. That's how I came to have that old cup that had come from that church when they disbanded the church and did away with all of it. My grandfather somehow came into ownership of that thing, and my grandmother had it for years, and I came across it at her house. I asked her about it, and she told me how she came to have it and all. She said I could have it. That was before I was ever married, probably when I was a late teenager or early twenties. She gave it to me, and I've kept it all these years. My daughter has it for her house now.

My grandfather was a commercial duck hunter too. Later on, after 1918, when the federal government prohibited the sale of migratory waterfowl, my grandfather became a commercial duck guide for Mr. Leroy Davis, who owned Monkey Island Hunt Club at that time. Mr. Davis owned the Whalehead Club before they sold it to Mr. Knight. Mr. Davis also owned a large enterprise known as Old Dominion Tobacco Company. His corporate offices were located in Norfolk. Mr. Davis wouldn't shoot any kind of duck except the canvasback. And he wouldn't let anyone else guide for him except my grandfather—that grandfather was the one who was killed in 1929. He was a commercial fisherman, as I said, and he and my grandmother's uncle fished together. This was in December; they were fishing and caught right many fish and were transporting them to Norfolk to a market late at night. They had an old vehicle that was ragged out, as most vehicles were in those days. They had a flat tire on the thing. My grandfather was changing the tire on Virginia Beach Boulevard and a truck struck him and killed him. He was born in 1868, and this was 1929, so he was about sixty years old.

Memories of Two Shipwrecks

One of the first memories of this beach that I still have a picture of in my mind had to do with the shipwreck of the *William H. Macy*, a schooner barge that went aground off Wash Woods beach in December 1915. In 1929, its remnants were still as plain as day. I remember it because this was the day my grandfather had been injured in that vehicle accident; he died the next day.

My dad was stationed at the False Cape Coast Guard Station at that time. They called him there to let him know that his father, my grandfather, had been injured and was in the hospital in Norfolk. We drove down to Corolla to get my grandmother. She lived right there at the Old Currituck Inlet at that time and had moved there just after the house had burned down that we lived in earlier. When we drove down here that morning—and it was a real cold morning—the sky was real red, and the sun was just coming up.

We could see that old *Macy*, bow stem and a lot of planking, hull and all were still visible then. It had been sixteen years since it went aground. A lot of planking and a lot of the ribs were still on that ship. I remember that thing being there, and I've seen it deteriorate over the years. The planks finally rotted away on it. The stem used to stand twelve or fifteen feet about the ground, the bow stem. Today people see it when it's exposed sometimes. It sits up about a foot and a half high now. Most people think it's a stump, but I have a friend in Knotts Island a couple of weeks ago who said he found a picture. He said it was a picture of the Macy when it first went aground. All three masts, the whole hull and everything is laying right there.

It was a lumber bark, and it was loaded with lumber, and it was on its way from South Carolina, probably Charleston to Baltimore, with a big load of lumber on it. People up there in the Wash Woods community picked up that lumber and built that church with it. People from Knotts Island came over here and gathered some of it up. That brand-new sawed lumber was all up and down the beach. John Gregory, who lived right at the south end of Knotts Island, built part of his house out of that lumber, and that house is still standing over at Knotts Island today. They would come over here and gather it up using horses and wagons—that's how a lot of things got built. In 1913, there weren't many vehicles of any kind, and everyone knew everyone, so if somebody from Knotts Island would come over here, they'd borrow somebody's horse and cart and get a load of that lumber, load it in their boat and take it back to Knotts Island. That was the *Macy*, and that picture shows her with all three masts in place and one sail still in place. If you've ever seen one of those maps of the Ghost Fleet, the *Macy* is listed on there.

Another old shipwreck, the *Plithia*, is commonly referred to as the marble wreck. It's up just north of the Virginia-Carolina line, about a quarter mile. It went aground in 1868. A lot of the hull is visible today at low tides and low water. It was loaded with huge blocks of Italian marble. It had two masts on it, from what I remember seeing of it. The masts have since been broken off and gone away.

The marble is still in the hold of that thing. We have a few in this community and a few from up in Sandbridge, as well, who come down here to go skin diving on that thing and spearfishing. They catch fish with spearguns, called triggerfish and sheepshead, down in that hull amongst all that marble. In about 1948 or 1949, three years after World War II,

This page: An exposed shipwreck on Currituck's Outer Banks. *Photo courtesy of Larry Riggs.*

Jesse Simkins from Norfolk, who was in the marine salvage business, had a surplus navy ship minesweeper, and he had mounted a crane on the fantail. He came down here with that thing, to the marble wreck, and let out anchor cable until he got close enough to it, until he could let the cable from the crane down into the hull. He had some divers with him. They went down into the hull and attached cable to some of those blocks of marble, and he lifted them out of there and was going to salvage the thing. He was of the opinion that they had quite a value.

They got two or three of those things out and loaded them on that minesweeper to take them away. A storm came along, and his boat dragged anchor, and he drifted down on the wreck. That was what broke one of the masts—the damage to the propeller on that minesweeper. The Coast Guard had to come to get him. He got into the harbor in Norfolk, tied that thing up and had some people come to appraise the marble. It wasn't worth a dime. The saltwater worms had pulverized that stuff. It was just as porous as could be. There is still quite a lot left in it. That thing has two hatches—hatch areas that make the hull inside accessible. It's surprising what a saltwater worm can do. I real often find conch shells that wash up on the beach, and if you look real closely, that thing has been pulverized with small holes drilled in it everywhere where saltwater worms have eaten that conch shell.

WORKING ON THE OUTER BANKS DURING THE GREAT DEPRESSION

I was right here during the Great Depression. I worked for fifty cents a day on an ice truck for Jethro Midgett down there in Nags Head for two summers, putting ice out, cutting it into blocks and putting it into iceboxes in all those Nags Head cottages built on pilings. [Recognized today as the "Unpainted Aristocracy," many of these rustically grand Nags Head homes are the archetype of the modern oceanfront Outer Banks home.] Some of those cottages would take a 150-pound block of ice, half a cake. A cake of ice weighed 320 pounds.

I'd cut that thing in half, put it in a canvas bag and put the two straps over my shoulders, and I weighed 150 pounds myself. I carried that 150 pounds of ice up those stairs and put it into those iceboxes. I worked for him for $0.50 a day, five days a week. He gave me $2.50. I could eat lunch in his mother's store. His mother owned a grocery store right next to the icehouse [near Jockey's Ridge today; the old store still stands]. I could have a thing of potted meat and a package of Saltine crackers and a Coca-Cola for lunch every day. He paid for that and paid me $0.50 an hour after. Coca-Cola, by the way, was a nickel in those days.

I could not be late to work in the morning because somebody would be waiting to get my job. Saturdays and Sundays I would go over to the sound side and catch soft crabs and sold them for sixty cents a dozen—and they had to be big for a hotel to buy it. I would pick up a little extra money on the weekends when the moon was right. That was a tough, tough time.

I remember the first pair of long pants I had in my life. My mother used to make me wear knickers all the time, and I hated those things. As soon as I would get out of her sight, I would jerk those things down to my ankles. I saved copper wire from all along the telephone lines up there all one summer. My dad sold it for me for junk that fall, and I got seven dollars and something for it—a whole summer of saving copper wire. I ordered two pairs of long pants from Sears and Roebuck out of a catalog for seven dollars. They had to be delivered to the post office in Oceana. The post office wasn't far from the school, and I walked all the way down to the post office every day to see if those pants had come in. My mother was madder than thunder at me because I spent my money for two pairs of long pants and wouldn't wear those knickers anymore.

During the Depression, some of the Coast Guard stations were placed in reserves, so to speak, in 1937, when money was short. Coast Guardsmen were given the choice: You can stay in the Coast Guard and take a reduction in rate and a reduction in pay, or we will let you out on an honorable discharge. Most of those Coast Guardsmen elected to take the reduction in rate and pay. My father, who at that time was a second-class boatswain mate, elected to go back to the rate known as surf man and stayed in the Coast Guard. His pay was reduced from ninety dollars a month to sixty dollars a month, or just two dollars a day. There were still some of the permanent Coast Guardsmen around, and I remember the Currituck Beach Station had two men stationed there. My great uncle was one of them. Those were hard times.

THE POST-WAR PLACE AND
BECOMING A MINESWEEPER SAILOR

You could count on both hands the number of people on this beach after World War II. Before the war, there were several communities along the Currituck Banks; I would say the village of Corolla had fifty or sixty residents, Seagull had about twenty-five residents, the Wash Woods Coast Guard area had fifteen or twenty people, maybe more than that. There were eight Coast Guardsmen there, and all of them had children. I daresay there were maybe thirty people in the Wash Woods area, most of them related to the Coast Guard or commercial fishermen and hunting guides that lived there.

Seagull at the time didn't have any Coast Guard–related families. That was all people dependent on their own various ventures, duck hunting, trapping, commercial fishing, so right at the end of the war, I came back here and worked at the Norfolk Naval Shipyard in diesel engineering.

It was there that I got a specialty in minesweepers—something the navy called a YMS ship. They were wooden hull ships at 125 feet long and 8 feet draft. They were wooden hulls for the simple reason that the wood would not attract a magnetic mine. The Japanese and the Germans had planted magnetic mines that were attracted to steel hull ships. These minesweepers were powered by two types of engines—one was by a Detroit engine known as an 82868A, which was an eight-cylinder engine. They were the main propulsion engines, and they had the same engine that drove a two-thousand-kilowatt generator that emitted the electrical charge on a steel cable that was attached to the ship. It has an apparatus on the end of it called a dolphin that they could set to run at a certain depth as the ship was running through the water.

Periodically, that generator would emit a charge on that steel cable that was on the dolphin and would snare a cable of a moored mine and the electrical charge would cut this cable and the mine would float to the surface. A crew would explode it with a shell fire from deck guns. The other engines they used were Cooper-Bessemer eight-cylinder engines, and they, too, were used for propulsion. The same motor that they used for main propulsion they used to drive those two-thousand-kilowatt generators.

Right after the war, a shrimping outfit from Morgan City, Louisiana, purchased three of those YMS minesweeping boats, which were declared surplus by the navy and were anchored in a tidal fleet up on the James River in Virginia. I don't know who put them in touch with me; apparently some of the naval personnel had been familiar with what I had been doing. They asked me if I would be interested in taking those three ships they had bought down to Morgan City, where they were going to outfit them for shrimp boats. I had two friends who were interested in joining me, and I accepted.

In the final analysis, we agreed to take those three minesweepers down the intercoastal waterway to Fort Pierce, Florida, and across Lake Okeechobee to Fort Myers and up the Gulf to Mobile Bay, to New Orleans and then to Morgan City. That was the only occasion I had to ever use my navigation skills that I may have obtained while Dad and I were studying Bowditch.

We took them down the James River and outfitted them over in Norfolk, where there were some ship handlers who sold supplies and those things. The navy had removed from those things this huge cable reel, which was located in a well in the stern of the boat, and as a result, it caused the boat to run down by the bow, and it would be drawing more than eight feet of water at the bow and about four feet at the stern—that made for an interesting ride.

While we were outfitting it in Norfolk, we rented some pumps and pumped those wells full of water to trim the thing up to make the bow come up and the stern go down; the wells held about twelve thousand gallons of water. The wells were really just a steel radius concave recession in the deck of the ship. That big reel had been set in there with two thousand feet of electrical cable mounted on it.

We left out of there, and because we only had three of us on each boat—I had two other guys on my boat and the others had some guys with them—we were prohibited from taking those things down the ocean because the maritime commission, or somebody, told us we couldn't do it. So, we left Norfolk going down the intracoastal waterway.

In 1940, the Atlantic Intracoastal Waterway had been dredged to eight feet depth maximum. A lot of filling had taken place since then. In our periodic stops, there would be times—well, in Fort Pierce, for example, the water got so shallow in the harbor there that we sat on the bottom for about three days before the tide came back and we could leave there to go on to Lake Okeechobee. That was quite a trip.

When we got to Morgan City, the shrimp outfit had a small shipyard, and they took the generator and the generator engine out of the generator compartment. Then we stayed there for about a week or ten days until they got that done. Then they wanted us to take them on across the intracoastal waterway to Orange, Texas, to a shipyard over there. At that shipyard, they installed refrigeration equipment where the generators had been, and that changed the profile quite a bit.

These shrimp people had fleets of—all in the Louisiana-Mississippi area—fifty-five-foot-long shrimp trawlers. The real shrimp grounds back then were off Vera Cruz, Mexico—that's where they were catching the best and largest shrimp. Those fifty-five-foot trawlers would leave Morgan City or wherever else on the Gulf Coast and go down to Vera Cruz, which took about a day and half to get there. They would load the cargo space in a matter of twelve to twenty-four hours and took a day and half to get back to get rid of them. They lost all that fishing time traveling. So, these ships I dealt were converted to what they referred to as "bum" boats. They refrigerated them and increased the cargo area by about ten times what those regular fifty-five-foot trawlers would carry.

As they would catch the fish or whatever down there, they would load the catch on this refrigerated ex-minesweeper until it was filled to capacity. Then they would go back to the processing plant, where the shrimp were processed, and the fifty-five-foot trawlers stayed onsite all the time. That was the reason for buying those things. We were about two months altogether from the time we picked those things up and got them over to Orange, Texas. That was where our responsibility ended, once we got them to the shipyard in Orange, Texas. We flew back home, as that was part of the deal.

Mr. Ocean Salvage

For centuries, the shores of the Outer Banks have seen wash up upon them all the things of the earth—from the natural wonders of the ecosystem to the jagged debris of broken ships to the treasures and trashes of a seaborne people. This flotsam and jetsam of our natural and man-made planet has always been a source of commerce and gathering for Outer Banks residents; not a few early local buildings were constructed with ocean debris. (The shipwreck timbers in the Corolla schoolhouse are plainly visible, for example.) In addition, many things—and people—tossed on the shores over time came to have a lasting impact on the lives of the shore collectors.

Over the years, I was just about the only one around to have enough heavy equipment to salvage heavy material from the ocean, and that led me into the salvage business. I have salvaged three sailboats and one fishing trawler out of the ocean. I had quite a story about one of those sailboats.

This one was in the 1980s. I was sitting in my house in Carova Beach one morning. It was raining; the wind was northeast, blowing, a typical September day early morning, and I was sitting at my table. I was having hot tea that morning, and I looked out at the ocean, and lo and behold, there was a sailboat right in the surf in front of my house, all leaned over on one beam.

I had just looked out there five minutes before that and it wasn't there. I got in my truck and drove over there right quick, and this thing is forty-two feet long and has a nine-and-a-half-ton keel in it. I rushed over there, and there was a man standing in the aft cockpit. It had a cabin on it and an open cockpit aft with the tiller and boom on the mast that swings back and forth. He was yelling and yelling. The wind was blowing, and the surf

Shipwreck on Currituck's Outer Banks. *Photo courtesy of Edward Ponton.*

was so loud, and it was hard to hear him. I asked him what he said. He said, "Can you get me off here?" I yelled back for him to jump overboard and walk ashore; it was only about waist deep. He was so frightened. He got off that boat, and he was soaking wet, and I noticed that his clothing looked different than most. It was a real heavy wool sweater turtleneck but a real different kind of wool, and his trousers looked a little different, and he spoke with a British accent.

We rode back over to my house, and he was shaking, cold and all. I got him inside. That goes back to the tea. That man told everyone since then that the first thing I said to him was "would you like a cup of tea?" He said he hadn't heard that since he left England. He had been living on this boat along with his wife and two children down in the islands—Martinique, I think, was the port he left from. But for several years, he had been transporting sailboats for other people. He was very adept at sailing sailboats. And he would pick up these boats from Newport, Rhode Island, or wherever up that way that very wealthy people owned, and take them to Florida for them, or to one of the islands in the Caribbean. The owner would fly down for their vacation and have their boat there too. When the vacation was over, they would fly home and get someone to sail the boat back home. That was what he had been doing for several years.

He didn't tell me the details, but I have come to understand over the years that Britain does not allow for a proceeding known as bankruptcy as we know it in this country. He had been an electrical engineer with a very affluent business at one time, and he was a fairly young man. I guess he was in his late thirties. Apparently, he got in financial trouble. I didn't inquire, and he didn't offer much information voluntarily. Just in the back of my mind, I felt that might be his situation. He just left England on this sailboat. He and his wife and children just lived down in the islands for several years.

His wife and two children had flown back to England, and he was sailing this boat from, I think, Martinique up to Annapolis, Maryland, where there is a big sailing center and lots of dealers take these boats on consignment and sell them for people. He had this thing on his boat called the automatic sailor. All sailboats moving about in public waters have the right-of-way over powerboats, so during the day, he would sleep because he knew any powerboats would get out of his way. He would set that automatic sailor on a course with the compass, and it was like a big rudder, but it was air controlled rather than water controlled. At daylight that morning, somewhere off of Corolla, he told me, he had set that automatic sailor on a course of north-northeast and was going to sleep during the day. This would probably take him up in the area of the entrance of the Chesapeake Bay by the time he awakened. At night, he stayed awake to be on the lookout for other ships that couldn't see him. Somehow or other, the automatic sailor malfunctioned off Carova Beach, and the thing did a 180-degree turn and came right back into the beach and landed right in front of my house.

Well, I was going to visit my daughter living in San Diego. I called the Coast Guard right away. They rushed up there and quickly searched the sailboat from bow to stern for contraband and drugs. They called up another Coast Guard boat from the Chesapeake Bay area. They came down with a big towing hawser, and they were going to try to tow it off at high water. They did attach a big towing hawser to it and floated it ashore with a buoy. The Coast Guardsman on shore retrieved it and attached it to this thing. This sailor's name was Martin, and I had come to know him during the day, and of course a great big crowd of people gathered up everywhere.

Everybody had to stop and talk about the sailboat and his shipwreck and all that business. The Coast Guard got the tow line attached to the cutter out in the ocean, started to pull him off and he was waving goodbye to everybody. They tried to pull that thing off stern first, and the first big wave over the sandbar swamped it. I had bought some gasoline pumps from my shop and had pumped all the water out of it so it would be afloat when the tide came back in, as the boat was only partially afloat, because it was going to be on its heel of that big keel underneath it.

Anyway, those waves swamped it right there. The cutter contacted the Coast Guardsman on the beach with the walkie-talkie and said to cut the hawser: "We're not going to pull it anymore. We're afraid we'll damage the boat." So, the Coast Guardsman cut that big towing hawser off with an axe. They left the boat laying there in the surf, tide coming in, about high water.

The guy got back overboard and got back on shore, and his boat was laying there banging in the surf. He wanted to know if there was anything I could do. I told him I was supposed to get a flight out of Norfolk Airport at 7:00 a.m. to go to California to visit my daughter for two weeks. I told him I would go get my crane at my barn. I still had two guys working for me that day. I asked them to stay with me. We got the crane, put a cable on the boat bow, put some skids and rollers on the ground and put a snatch bob on it so I could get a double purchase on it. Fortunately, I began to move it out of the surf and up on the beach. I guess it took us about four hours to get that thing far enough up on the beach that another high water wouldn't reach it. By then it was late at night. Folks were shining automobile lights down there so we could see to work. I told Martin I had to get out of there and go get packed. I told Martin that here was my house, help yourself, I'll call you from California to see if you need anything. First time I had ever seen the man in my life.

The next morning, I got my flight and went to California. I called him once or twice. He said he was getting along fine, doing some things to the boat, taking some clothes out of it, drying stuff and salvaging paperwork. I came back from California, drove up to my house and here is a lady and two little children in the house. She introduced herself as Mrs. Martin, and these were her two boys. It turned out, Martin told me, he didn't have any money, and he didn't know what to do.

I had given him some cash, told him that would buy him something to eat, and whatever is here, help yourself until I get back. When I got back later on, folks told me someone took him to up the beach and he deposited $6,000 in a bank up there. He didn't tell me the truth about that, but anyway, he had sent for his wife and children soon after I went to California. They were set up in my house when I got back. I had a mobile home down at my shop and barn that sometimes one of the employees would stay in rather than transport them back and forth up the beach. Nobody was there at the time, so I told Martin that he and his wife and children could stay over there. There was water and electricity and all you need for a short time.

In the meantime, he picked up a little Volkswagen from somebody in the neighborhood, and he was driving it.

Several weeks had gone by, and I asked him what he could do. He said a little bit of this and a little bit of that. I told him I had a lot of work to do if he wanted to do some of it. At that time, I was putting up sand fence for the developers all up in Swan Beach, North Swan, Carova, at Whalehead, everywhere. I was charging them so much per roll, and I was buying the sand fence in tractor trailer loads from the factory down in Georgia. They would deliver it to Sandbridge to me, and I was reloading it up there and bringing it down here on trailers with floatation tires on them. I would bring one hundred rolls of sand fencing at a time. I told him if he wanted to start putting up sand fencing, I would pay him, just as I was paying these other guys who were working for me. I had more than the other guys could get done. He started putting up sand fence for me, and to make a long story short, he and his wife and children stayed with me there for three years.

Those children were enrolled in a school in Kitty Hawk. When they were tested to see what their accomplishments were and what grade to place them in, they were about two grades ahead of the other children in their age group. They were smart as briers, those two little boys. And their mother, it turned out, was a registered nurse. They could live anywhere under any kind of circumstances. But they lived back over at that horse barn, and he would take those two little boys over to Corolla, and they would catch the school bus to Kitty Hawk. He could talk to anybody.

Eventually, his wife went back to England with the two little boys. He came down to Duck to Britt Realty. He made a deal with them to teach sailing and started a school teaching people to sail sailboats. I guess that went on for a year or two. His big sailboat was still laying on the beach right in front of my house. He said he didn't know how to get it out of there. I said, "Well it's not hurting anybody. We'll see if we can find some way to move it one day." Soon after that, there was a guy from over in Camden County moving houses, Julian Bray. Julian was moving a house within Carova Beach, and he had his equipment up there. I had known Julian for a long time. I asked Julian to come look at this boat to see if we could get it off the beach. He said yes. We would have to take the mast out of it, but he said when he got through moving the house, he would come down and load it. Martin came back up there, took the mast out of the thing, lashed it to the hull and all the other sailing equipment. Julian loaded it up on the beams and dollies and took it right off the beach, through Corolla, across the bridge, over the mainland to Centerville Turnpike and the intracoastal waterway up in

Shipwreck on Currituck's Outer Banks. *Photo courtesy of Edward Ponton.*

Chesapeake. He unloaded it up there. Martin left his sailing lessons business down there and called me two or three times with something or another he wanted me to help him with on his boat.

The last time I went up there he had put it in the water, got the little auxiliary motor going—everything on it was English—got that motor going, got the mast back in it and all the sails rigged. He said, "I'm going on to Annapolis, but I'm coming back to teach more sailing." I never heard from Martin again. I don't know what in the world happened to him.

The *Virginian Pilot* did several articles on that sailboat. I'm sure they have a lot of information in their files up there. People would come by for a long time and see that boat laying up there next to the dunes. People would stop and walk all around that boat. Nobody ever vandalized it or did anything to it.

THE ONE-DOLLAR SHRIMP TRAWLER

I salvaged a shrimp trawler up in Back Bay that belonged to a Vietnamese family. They encountered a storm off Virginia Beach, and fortunately, there was another shrimp trawler that transferred them, and it went aground up in the Back Bay Wildlife Refuge. The Fish and Wildlife Service told them they had to get it out of there. They brought the other shrimp boat down. It was cold in the winter. One of the crewmen tied a rope around his waist, and the boat came in as close to shore as it dared without going aground. That guy jumped overboard to swim ashore with that rope, and they were going to pull a longer rope in and tie it to the shrimp trawler, and at high water, they were going to try to tow it back out. They didn't see him on the shore, and when they pulled the rope back, he wasn't on it. The rope came loose, and he drowned. They found the body about two months later on the beach. They asked me if I could get that shrimp trawler out of the refuge for them, and I told them yes. They wanted to know how much I would charge. They said they couldn't pay that much, and I told them I couldn't do it for any less. I had to hire men and use my crane, get it up out of the ocean, get steel beams under it and dollies and all that stuff to transport it. They said, well, what can we do? I don't know anyone else that wants to do it. They said can we give you that boat? I said on one condition. I'm going to pay you one dollar for it, and you transfer the ownership papers to me because I don't want to be stuck with something that I don't own. I gave them a dollar for it and got it up out of the ocean and towed it down to where my barn was at that time and stripped it. It had a diesel motor in it, hydraulic wenches in it and a bunch of other stuff that I stripped and sold. I had a junk man come over and cut the steel hull. It was sixty-eight feet long. I had him cut it away and sell it for junk. I sold the motor. I still have the propeller out of it.

LIVESTOCK ON THE OUTER BANKS

After the war, I lived in the Oceana [Virginia] area. It was all rural at that time. In 1947, I became involved in the refrigeration and air conditioning sales and service business—I opened my own business in Oceana. In 1952, the Korean War started. The government froze all copper, so our industry couldn't get any copper except that which was used in the manufacture of military equipment. I sold my refrigeration business, the land, the shop and the inventory and came back to the Outer Banks permanently. I bought five hundred acres of land in what is today the Carova Beach subdivision area. I leased thirty-five acres from the Swan Island Hunt Club, who were the people who owned the adjoining property, and I became involved in the livestock industry.

Back on the Outer Banks, the livestock industry at that time was prolific. It was largely bovine or cattle herds and sheep herds. All the way down through Nags Head, as far as Oregon Inlet, there were herds of cattle and sheep that roamed at large. They were owned by different individuals who used or traded them for all kinds of things. I got into that business and stayed in it for a long time.

At that time, there were two ways of identifying whose cattle was whose. The most popular method of identifying was what was known as an earmark. You would take the cow's ear—or the ear of a pig or a sheep—and make your mark as a kind of record of ownership. I recorded the last earmark record with the Register of Deeds Office in Currituck County in 1951 or 1952.

Those earmarks were handed down from one member of a family to another. And my grandmother transferred that earmark to me, and I recorded it with the Register of Deeds Office in 1952, I think. These earmarks were very definitive. They were also used in the western United States, as well as brands. So far as I can remember, there were only two brands used on this Outer Banks, Currituck County. A man by the name of Williams used a simple branding iron with a *W*, his initial, and he branded most of his livestock on the shoulder. I recorded a brand that was known as a "B in a Box." It was just a square box with the letter *B* in the center of it. I branded my livestock on the hip. But the earmark defined—if you can picture the ear of an animal—was an underkeel of the right ear and an underkeel of the left. That meant the very point of the ear was cut off, so it was square. That was known as a crap. And an underkeel was a *V* in the bottom of the ear, and that was the mark that I recorded that belonged to my grandmother back in the 1800s. They called them smooth crap both ears; that would be the tips of both ears would be cut off and that earmark would belong to one family. Another mark would be a swallowfork. Instead of a point on the ear, you converted it to a *V*.

There were lots of variations to those kinds of marks going back a long time—underslope, underkeel, overkeel, swallowfork and crap—that's cattle language. One might refer to the left ear, one to the right ear, one might refer to both ears and then there was another mark that some people used known as the doo-lap. The part of the cow's skin portion was always very loose, and they would just slice it and let it hang. It would heal again after the mark was done, and that was known as a doo-lap. Some folks recorded these with the county, and some folks didn't. These marks were written out in the deeds and included a picture as I described it.

Cattle and Livestock Dipping

I have a picture of the last real roundup of cattle that were roaming at large on this Currituck beach. It was taken in 1949, in August. It was a front-page article in the *Virginian Pilot*. That picture shows a group of riders herding a herd of cattle to a corral. Dr. Fink was a veterinarian from Elizabeth City, and the U.S. Department of Agriculture adopted this regulation or law back in the late 1920s that created all these dipping vats that they funded.

The idea was to eradicate the ticks on all the livestock. In each area where there were dipping vats, the corralling of the livestock was scheduled for a certain day, and there had to be a veterinarian there to inspect all the livestock. Dr. Fink used to come here from Elizabeth City. Every time we would herd up these cattle and sheep and horses, we had to dip everything, even dogs. If a kid would come around with a dog, Dr. Fink would make him put it in that dipping vat.

That dipping vat was filled with water, fish oil and sulfur to kill the ticks. The vat was made out of concrete and there were steps made in it so the cattle could get out without slipping and falling. There is one today that sits down there by itself on the old Linwood Dudley tract. There were a bunch of those old dipping vats. It's before you get to where Cameron Gray is on the right—sitting over there toward the marsh. There is one up there at the site of the old False Cape Hunt Club on Mr. Ike Edwards's property too. We had a dipping vat there. We had a dipping vat where Little Island Station is today, up in Sandbridge, one in Corolla, one in Pine Island when Dr. Baum owned it. Kitty Hawk Woods had a couple or three, and back in Nags Head Woods, there were more. Most of them have been destroyed. The one here is the only one I know left in Currituck County. They had dipping vats on the mainland as well.

There were lots of cattle on this beach, and I had the last herd. Lots of people owned cattle here. We did a cattle roundup every year, usually in June, July or August. The northernmost corrals were up in what is known today as False Cape State Park. We rounded up cattle from there all the way to the village of Corolla. Captain Lewark had corrals here and a big old dipping vat. There was one right here in Corolla behind what is now the Villages of Ocean Hill. Captain Hump Lewark said he owned an acre of land there and built his corrals there and had the dipping vat there. Helen Parker gave the deed to the property to the county years ago. She was tired of paying taxes on it.

When we would conduct the cattle drives on the beaches, this was us getting the herd ready for market. We sold the feeder calves to go in feed lots, and some of the calves were veal—175-pound calves. We did the roundups on horseback. I remember that Nags Head Woods had two large herds of cattle. One belonged to Marshall Tillett and the other belonged to Captain Bill Partridge.

All the cattlemen knew each other. I bought up all the last herds of cattle. I bought Mr. Lloyd O'Neal's herd, Mr. Cason's herd, Mr. Linwood Dudley's herd and Mr. Alton James's herd. As they became older and got out of the business, I bought their herds. My grandfather had a herd of cattle. My grandmother continued that after he died. My dad's middle brother had a herd of cattle, but my dad was in the Coast Guard and so was his younger brother, so they were never involved in the cattle business until my dad retired. Then he was associated in it with me. I went into the livestock business here after the war. My dad was the only help I had. At the peak of the time I was involved in the livestock industry, I owned about three hundred head of cattle. I owned the last commercial cattle herd on the Outer Banks. I disbursed it in about 1996 by selling most of my cattle.

I operated what was known as a cow-calf operation. I just raised the calf to feeder calf weights and sold them to the feedlots for finishing. A feedlot would want calves weighing 450 pounds max. Other years, when grain was high, they would want the cow-calf operator to grow the calf to 500 or 600 pounds so they wouldn't have it in the feedlot so long on the high-priced grain. The market varied from year to year. I transported the cattle. Some of them I sold in Smithfield, Virginia, at the livestock market. Some I sold to a Virginia Packing Company in Suffolk, Virginia, who was a broker for some feedlots, and he would buy feeder cattle and transfer them to the feedlots. And I sold some cattle in Siler City, North Carolina, and some in Rocky Mount and some in Elizabeth City over the years. It just depended on the market.

For transportation in later years, I used what we called a goose-neck stock trailer, thirty-two feet long. It would transport about twelve grown animals and about fifteen to eighteen feeder calves. But I would, as a rule, sell a group of twenty-five to forty to a feedlot, and it would take about four or five trips to deliver all of them. My route was straight up into Virginia. That's how I have a permit from the Department of Interior that allows me to drive from here up into Sandbridge up in Virginia Beach.

When I got started after the war, I bought a herd of my own in 1948, about fifteen or twenty cattle. I blended them into my grandmother and grandfather's herd and then I started buying more cattle. I bought thirty or forty cattle from Mr. Dudley. Mr. Roy O'Neal had about twenty or thirty head of cattle down by Lewark Hill. I bought all his cattle. Lundy Cason had about twenty-five head of cattle out there on Swan Island. He died and I bought his herd from his wife. I bought all my uncle's cattle after he came down with cancer. He still had about fifty or seventy-five head of cattle, and I bought all of them before he died.

Then the development and the subdivisions came, and as these folks moved in from other places, they started objecting to everything. I had to start fencing. There was a day when I put 1,100 fence posts in the ground in one day.

At one time, I had a llama, a little old Sicilian donk and a couple of little mule foals, two black Angus cows, a bunch of peacocks, a bunch of chickens, some turkeys, one hog. The hog's name was Arnold. I took him to the livestock sale and sold him. He weighed 804 pounds. I had a herd of four hundred goats at one time. Not many people had acquired a taste for goat, but I am very fond of it. After I didn't have goats anymore, I would buy a goat and barbeque it.

I also had a herd of buffalo. I started with three buffalo, and I got my herd up to fifteen at one time, but I had a big buffalo bull that liked Corolla. That joker would wander off down there—you could put him in a boxcar—and he would find a way to get out. He would get out of that pasture up there, and he would come all the way down to Corolla, and he would be out there on those manicured lawns in Corolla Light, and I'd come down there to get him, and the first two or three times I came down

Beach grass along Currituck's Outer Banks. *Photo courtesy of Larry Riggs.*

on a horse to get him and it would take half or three-fourths of that day, so the next time, finally, I took my horse home, got my pick-up truck and brought my two dogs with me—I had an Australian shepherd and an Australian heeler—and I'd find that buffalo around somebody's house, and I'd put those two dogs on him, and they'd get him over to the ocean, and he would go till he was tired, then he'd walk right out in the ocean and just stand there. Waves would break over him, and he would just stand there. I'd sit up on the beach, and the dogs would come get in the truck and the buffalo would be in the ocean. He'd stay there nigh thirty minutes before he would come ashore. He'd come out of the water up on the beach, and I'd get the dogs on him again, take him up the beach another mile or two and he would get tired and go back in the ocean.

STORMS AND HIGH WATERS

Human time takes place not in hours or minutes but in the stories we tell. As so often happens, our own best stories often take place in the larger backgrounds of adversity—a kind of where-we-were-when shared reference that together hangs in our hearts like a star that guides us. Perhaps no other kind of adversity better defines the Outer Banks than the myriad storms that have angrily claimed and unclaimed the coast over the centuries. Depending on your age and your local roots, native Outer Bankers will often plot their lives, chart-like, along storm tracks and memories—the storms of '33, Hurricane Hazel, the Ash Wednesday Storm or the more recent storms of Hurricane Irene, Florence or Dorian all start conversations of common bonds. Older Outer Banks homes often have Sharpie-style flood markings along the home's exterior of different storm high-water marks. Many of these dramatic events have spurred government actions that brought more development in some way—where there is great need, the government has usually acted along the shores whether it is live-saving, infrastructure or, in modern days, even beach renourishment.

No matter the year or floodwaters, however, each storm in the end transitions from a weather story to a people story as it makes landfall in our lives. As Mr. Ernie shares, we come to be defined by them as they move across our memories as channel markers to our journey.

1933 Storms

We had two storms in 1933—one the last week in August and one the second week of September. Most folks would say 1933 Hurricane, but there were really two of them back-to-back just three weeks apart. In the second storm of 1933, the ocean moved clean across the beaches and went all the way to Back Bay and Currituck Sound. The reason for that was because all the dune line had disappeared, and everything was flat from the previous hurricane a few weeks earlier. Those back-to-back storms are to be feared.

At the time, my dad was in the Coast Guard, stationed at the False Cape Station, and we lived right there. He also had a commercial fishing operation that he did when he was off duty. He had a dory and a net and all that stuff. You didn't have any trailers for dorys back then—you just dragged them around. That afternoon before dark, my dad brought his dory over from the ocean. People used to leave their dorys and nets and everything right out there on the ocean, and nobody ever bothered with anything back in those days. You could leave your truck and everything, sit around, and nobody would bother it. My dad brought his dory back from the ocean—actually almost floated it over here since everything was so flooded. Just before dark, the ocean was getting so bad, he put the bow of the dory in the back door of the house. My mother, my sister was five, my brother was two years old and I was eight. My dad put them and my grandmother in the dory. The current was going down the road that led to Back Bay where the False Cape Hunt Club was. All dad did was stay on the stern of that dory overboard and guided it all the way down that roadway. The tide took us all the way back to the high ground at the False Cape Hunt Club. We got out of the dory back there and spent that night. He could guide all that way by wading. There were some trees on either side of the roadway or cart path. That area up in the False Cape is more stable than down in this area. The sound is so close to the ocean down in this area.

The Violence and Sadness of the Ash Wednesday Storm

The well-documented Ash Wednesday Storm is perhaps the most famous storm to ever impact the Outer Banks. Making landfall in 1962, the storm itself affected much of the East Coast of the United States, although locally, it remains famous for three key reasons: 1) it was not a hurricane,

2) it was largely a surprise and 3) the terrific ocean overwash. The storm's lasting effects even today remind us that we live in a fragile place and, above all, to keep an unfailing weather eye on the ocean and the currents.

My grandmother died in the Ash Wednesday Storm in 1962 and so did Griggs O'Neal's mother, although not in the same house. Griggs's homeplace is right behind the current-day Currituck Beach Coast Guard Station. In short, my uncle always said that the storm simply came in the front door and went out the back.

At the height of that famous storm, the wind and water moved my grandmother's house almost a quarter mile; the tide picked it right off the foundation and carried it with my grandmother, my uncle and his wife all inside. That was my father's mother, Margaret Beasley Bowden. She lived up near the old Currituck Inlet near the original site of the Penny's Hill Coast Guard Station.

My grandmother was eighty-four, of course, and they kept her afloat during the height of the storm on a mattress. She died right there during that storm but not due to drowning—she died of exposure and stress and all that stuff. They had to leave when it became daylight, and there was still heavy activity in the water. The tide moved her off her bed, and she was lying behind her bed when I went in the house to get her. I got her up out of the water. The water was still deep in the house. I got her on her bed and wrapped her in a bed quilt. The Coast Guard helped me get her out of the house. My dad waited out on the shoreline. It was his mother, of course. We waded in deep water all the way out to the berm, as the dunes were simply gone. My uncle and his wife left the house earlier at daylight and sought higher ground.

During the storm, I was working at the livestock market in Elizabeth City—Bright Tatum Livestock Market out on Body Road in Elizabeth City. I owned a piece of it at one time. Sales were held every Monday, and I went to the livestock sale. They sold cattle, pigs, sheep and everything there. I would be there on Mondays, and I ran the office. We had two ladies and another man who worked up there with us. We did all the billings and all the collections right there on Mondays. Usually, I'd get out of that sale, depending on how large the sale was, around seven o'clock at night until eleven if you had a big sale. Sometimes I would leave that sale at night and drive to Rocky Mount to Gus Lancaster's livestock market. His sales were on Tuesday. On this occasion I had gone to Rocky Mount on Monday night. I called my dad from up there. He was at the Wash Woods Coast Guard Station that had a phone, an old crank thing, the only telephones on the beach at that time. I called my dad just checking in with him. He said the ocean was getting terrible. He said it had been building since yesterday and said it was really getting rough. This was on Tuesday afternoon. I said, "Well, this was a short sale. I'll be getting out of here pretty soon, and I'm going to come on back tonight." I left Rocky Mount around nine to ten o'clock. When I got to Elizabeth City, there was all this snow and ice. Back in those days, the telephone lines from Elizabeth City to Shawboro were the same as the Coast Guard telephone lines here—bare copper wire on long insulators up on poles on crossarms with insulators on them. When I got between Camden and Shawboro, all that open land, those telephone poles were all laid out in the fields, and the telephone lines were all broken off. That told me how hard the wind had been blowing.

I always come through Virginia, coming back to the beach. I got up into rural Virginia Beach, and it was really some kind of bad. And that storm, the worst of it took place after midnight on Tuesday night. I couldn't reach my dad and couldn't get through. I got up to Sandbridge, and they had evacuated all of Sandbridge. I got up to old Princess Anne County—in those days it hadn't merged into a city. There was a policeman there who set up a roadblock and wouldn't let anyone come into Sandbridge. I knew him. He was a lieutenant on the police force. Bradshaw was his last name. He said he couldn't let me go down the beach, that lights were out everywhere, and all was dark. I said I wasn't going all the way back to Virginia Beach, so I would just sit here in my truck. He said I could sit in the police car with him. So, I sat in the car with him. Sometime about daylight the next morning, he had a radio call to respond to an accident back up the road. He asked me to go along, and I said no, I would stay here. As soon as he got gone, I left for the beach.

It was low water on the beach right then, but the waves were huge. I got down to the Little Island Coast Guard Station. There was an inlet, and the ocean was just running into Back Bay. On the edge of that inlet, I saw about that much of the top of a Coast Guard Power Wagon. The ocean had washed that thing into the inlet, and of course, the crew was all gone; they had abandoned the Coast Guard station. I waited about two hours or so, and I realized that I could go out into the edge of the ocean with my truck and get by that inlet when a wave went down, and that's what I did. I found two other inlets between there and the Wash Woods Coast Guard Station. The primary dune was all gone. I was driving on a little berm out front and back where all the subdivision is today. There was nothing but water everywhere. You could look right over to Knotts Island and see the houses just as clear as day.

I got down to the Wash Woods Station, and there was so much water behind that berm I couldn't drive over there. I had to wade in water above my knees. There was water all around the Coast Guard station, two or three feet deep. My dad was not there. We had that big boathouse on the north side of the building, so I went out there. His truck was in there. He kept it parked in the old boathouse. I went out to the horse barns, which were out beyond the Coast Guard station, and the horses were all gone. I had maybe been there twenty or thirty minutes when my dad came in riding that sorrel horse he had. He said he had left about dark the night before after I had talked to him. He said, "The water was pooling up all around here, and I didn't know where I could go with my truck." He was afraid he would get stalled in one of those deep holes somewhere. I had several registered Appaloosa horses back in the barn. He said, "I turned your horses out." I said that was alright; they would come back. He said he rode his horse way down in the woods, way over next to Knotts Island Bay. He took some type of rain-proof tarp and spent the night in the woods over there with his horse.

The next morning, he went out to where my grandmother and my uncle lived near the state line, and my uncle and his wife were there. He told my dad that my grandmother had died during the night. Our neighbor Mrs. O'Neal had died during the night as well. They lived not far apart, a few hundred feet. Dad rode on back over there. There are several houses that were covered under that sand dune. One that is now being exposed is the Beasley house. The first I saw of it, Gerald Friedman and Larry Riggs, prior to them selling that marshland to the Department of Interior, wanted to see the residual of Swan Beach that they never had developed. I met them and drove them right up over that dune that falls right down over that marsh. As we were driving along, people had been driving on top of that dune anyway; I was following their tracks. I looked out the window and I saw a few bricks just

A beach house on Currituck's Outer Banks. *Photo courtesy of Larry Riggs.*

like that hearth. It was the chimney of old man Beasley's house just being exposed. That is the December 1962 issue. Most people think of the Ash Wednesday Storm as being concentrated right here on the Outer Banks. We didn't suffer any damage compared to what happened to the Delmarva Peninsula, New Jersey, and the Eastern Shore of Virginia and even Virginia Beach proper. Gosh, Virginia Beach proper along the oceanfront was about demolished. All those huge windows in motels were all broken out.

THE CONUNDRUM OF COASTAL DEVELOPMENT

COUNTY GOVERNMENT, DEVELOPMENT AND EARLY TOURISM ON THE CURRITUCK OUTER BANKS

In the late '60s, the Outer Banks community began to see the first signs of commercial development as a reflection of tourism, although real construction wouldn't take place until the early 1980s. As in many places across the country, a thing has to be fine indeed to not have two sides and balancing the right kinds of private property development with shared protection of the natural environment sparks intense conversation, downright disagreement and outright anger in many ways. Development is always a partnership, in a sense, between private interests, government entities both elected and non-elected, and individual citizens who maintain property rights either in concert with or in opposition to community responsibility. Development, especially along the fragile Outer Banks, has always been a fine balance, but its story—and critically the people involved—are particularly important to understanding the place and its people today. Of note, many of our projects around transportation today, to include the ballyhooed Mid-County Bridge, are the continuance of many decades of efforts to better connect the Currituck Outer Banks to the world beyond.

In 1954, Congress deeded to the State of Virginia a fifty-five-foot-wide easement through the Back Bay Refuge for the purpose of constructing an all-weather road that would connect to a highway in North Carolina at the Virginia–North Carolina state line. As a result of the right-of-way that was deeded to Virginia, the two states created what was known as a bistate commission. It was composed of three members from each state. The chairman of the North Carolina Commission was a man named Merle Evans, who was commissioner of highways in North Carolina. Our local representative on that commission, since the road was to connect in Currituck County, was Baxter Williams.

Baxter was also on the board of education and later served with me on the board of commissioners for two terms. Our counterpart, the Virginia chairman, was a man named Sidney Banks who was a well-known businessman in the old town of Virginia Beach and owned, at one time, the Cavalier Hotel—Cavalier on the hill, we called it.

Mr. Paul Brown, who was a member of the board of supervisors in Virginia—like we have the county commissioners—also played a key role. He lived down in the lower Princess Anne County area and was a very influential farmer, landowner and had always been involved in local government things.

I don't remember the other members; I just remember two from each commission. The road was actually surveyed down to the village of Duck, and I don't know how much farther. It was to be known as an ocean highway connecting the highway in Virginia to the highway in North Carolina. Virginia proposed a toll road. North Carolina law, it turned out—after all this business had gone through, the surveying and what not—prohibits the connection of a toll road to a public highway in North Carolina, so that killed that highway in 1955.

As time went on, people began to utilize the beach for driving down from Virginia for recreational purposes. People started coming to camp on the beach and spend the weekend along the beach. The area of Penny's Hill was wide open and quite popular—there could easily be one hundred cars there on a weekend to include all kinds of hill-climbing vehicles people built. People would bring grills, families and all-ages children would be there as well. While this was a great example of early Outer Banks tourism, it brought with it problems as well.

The traffic on the beach reached a point where the federal government in the [Virginia] Back Bay Wildlife Refuge didn't appreciate it. It's important to note that three coastal states in the United States recognize mean low water to be the extent of a property owner's ownership—Massachusetts, Virginia and Georgia. All the other states, including North Carolina, recognized the mean high water as the extent of a property owner's rights. The U.S. Department of Interior—through the U.S. Fish and Wildlife Service—moved on the strength of that law. They announced their intent to eliminate all vehicular traffic on the beach through the Back Bay Wildlife Refuge, but they didn't do that until Congress repealed that fifty-five-foot easement through the Back Bay Refuge.

Virginia had not utilized it from 1954 to 1970. About 1970, the Fish and Wildlife Service announced their intent to restrict traffic. That went through a long legal process, about three or four years in the courts. The developers, by that time, had begun developing these subdivisions, and they were transporting potential buyers down the beach from Sandbridge [the coastal community neighbor north of Carova in Virginia; as the crow flies about a twenty-minute modern day drive if it were possible, which it is not due to the vehicle protections in the Refuge]. That would certainly put a burden on them if they couldn't transport people. They went so far as to buy an amphibious plane at one time—but never utilized it—to ferry people down to the Corolla area and transport them back, up and down the beach from Corolla to sell these properties.

The final resolution of the litigation was the Fourth Circuit of Appeals, which upheld Judge John McKinzie's First District Federal Court ruling. That ruling was that the Fish and Wildlife Service did own the land to mean low water and that they could control any activities on that tidal beach. The developers appealed again to gain some time to sell as many lots as they could. The Fourth Circuit upheld it on appeal. The Fish and Wildlife Service initiated their permit system in 1974. Judge McKinzie's ruling stated that, in addition to recognizing ownership, long-term permanent residents of the Currituck Outer Banks had established certain inherent rights that the Fish and Wildlife Service must address in their rules-making process. That went on for a year or two, and the first accommodations were to those who were permanent residents down here as of December 1976 or before, and that was later amended to December 1980.

The first rule said anybody living from the Currituck Beach Lighthouse to the Virginia–North Carolina line as of 1976 would receive a permit. Jesse Helms was the patron of that bill in Congress, and it survived all the conflict that it created and became law. During the period of development from 1967 until 1974, when the permit process started, the developers were telling the people that there would be a road constructed from Virginia to North Carolina—or access eventually. Well, in 1974, the ruling shot all of that down of course. The developers had to stop putting that information in their

A beach house on Currituck's Outer Banks. *Photo courtesy of Larry Riggs.*

information packet. I saw this development coming into something I didn't really appreciate. They were moving a lot of mobile homes into the Carova Beach and Swan Beach subdivision, and by and large, they were older mobile homes that people were using for weekends and summer vacation things. The county, at the time, did not have a building code at all. If you were going to build a house in Currituck County on the mainland or beach in those days, you went to Mickey Dozier, the tax supervisor, and told him you wanted to build a house. Mickey would fill out this little permit. You would give him one dollar. He told you when you finished the house to come back, and he would go look at it and place a value on it for tax purposes. You could build anything you wanted to build back in those days. I prevailed upon the county in 1972 to stop the influx of those mobile homes to the Currituck Outer Banks, and they did—that was before I was a member of the board of commissioners. I saw this building going on that was dangerous, and I knew that access was not coming from the north and people had been—I won't say they were duped because it was legal at the time—wrong in thinking they'd have access from the north.

Developers were making it easy as the debate went on though; $100 down and $50 each month got you an oceanfront lot selling for $8,500. [Today, many oceanfront lots sell for more than $1 million.] Interior lots were down as much as $600 if you bought them in multiples. If you bought as many as six, you could buy them for $400 each. The far interior prices varied with canal lots selling, at the time, for $4,500. It was an easy payment thing; everything was sold on contract. Nothing was sold by metes and bounds and deeds. Notes or deeds of trust and those things didn't take place. It was so much easier for the developers to take it back on a contract than it would be if he had a note and a deed of trust if you defaulted. And they experienced some defaults, I'm sure, over the years.

Subdividing the Currituck Outer Banks

The subdivisions and lot sales and people who were interested in improving those lots made all the difference. It was raw land; not many improved lots were being sold at that time. Retirees, by and large, improved the lots. There was very little employment except for those working for developers. Most of the development these people did was done on paper, while little real physical development was actually done. The Whalehead subdivision was done on paper, as all these subdivisions were, until Mr. Dick Brindley came along. I recognize him as the patriarch of modern-day development we see here now. Planned physical development was done under Mr. Brindley.

For example, the Whalehead subdivision was done in a grid design with parallel streets, cross streets, everything divided up into 600-foot increments or 1,200-foot increments. Everything the same. But when Mr. Brindley came along, he began to design a subdivision that had far more amenities than we had seen prior to that. He was doing real building with a vision for the future. His company was actually building some buildings and selling the lot with the building in place. None of that ever happened in Whalehead—that was mostly raw land.

The developers never built a house in Whalehead to sell. They sold the raw lot, and somebody else did the construction and design. Mr. Brindley sure set the tone for a lot of the development we see here today. The Ocean Hill and the Villages at Ocean Hill was kind of a grid type of thing that Mr. Gerald Friedman did; at one time, I think he owned a half mile on the sound in Corolla.

In considering his subdivision and public hearing, I asked him what he was going to do with that property back on the bay. It is separated by the "old pole road," as we referred to it. I said a good bit of it didn't lend itself to development, but it does have some high ground in places. He said he hadn't thought about it. I suggested he give that piece to the county; it was so remote from the rest of the subdivision. He would find it difficult to incorporate it into the rest of the development as it goes on. He said he didn't have any problem with that. He deeded the county fifty acres back there—half mile of sound front. The southern boundary was what we call Net Scaffle Creek, and it was pretty good deep water coming right in from the sound. We had the land, and I suggested to the county that we would need that land somewhere down the line for recreation or public utilities or wastewater treatment plant or something. And they all agreed with me.

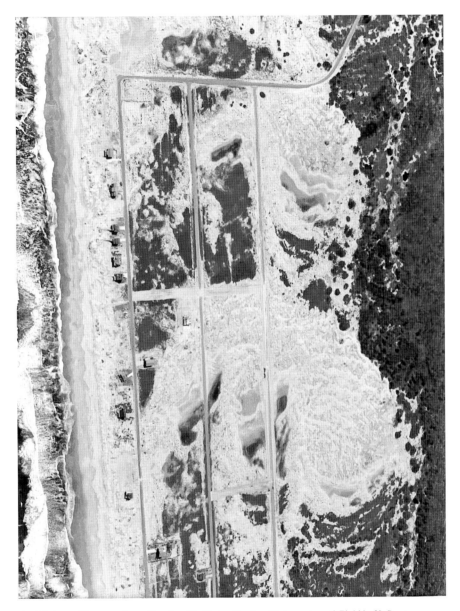

Aerial shot of homes along Currituck's Outer Banks. *Photo courtesy of Twiddy & Company.*

About four years later, along came a new board—Wilson Snowden, Frances Walker. That was along about the time Lady Bird Johnson was promoting all this beautification all across the country, and Frances Walker keynoted on that, and Wilson Snowden was very interested in Monkey

Island. They proposed to trade the fifty acres and half mile shoreline to the federal government, who had purchased the Monkey Island compound from the nature conservancy.

They wanted to trade it to the Fish and Wildlife Service for Monkey Island. By then, I was a commissioner, and I voted against it. I didn't like it. I thought we needed this thing, and there were a lot of problems with Monkey Island. Erosion had already cut it in half. Mr. George Twiford was the caretaker there in the early 1950s. I bulkheaded all the east side of Monkey Island for the owners at that time. The owners were William and Ed Lynch from Greensboro. They were large tobacco warehouse people, and they had bought the Monkey Island property, and a lot of erosion was taking place on the east side. They had Mr. George get somebody to bulkhead it, and I bid on it and got the job. By the time they wanted to trade it off, the bulkhead was twenty feet out in the water because nobody had bothered to maintain it; nobody had built more bulkhead after William and Ed sold it, so the tide got in behind it and eroded it.

They said they wanted to use it as an education center and take high school children over there. I asked them if they realized the liability you would incur by transporting children over there across that water. They were talking about a pontoon boat to bring those children over there. The island would require so much maintenance to ever bring it up to where it would be acceptable to anybody. They were bound and determined to do it, and they did over my vote. They traded off that fifty acres and shoreline. A condition of the trade was—put in by the Fish and Wildlife Service—you must make forty-seven reasonable improvements to Monkey Island within a ten-year period, or it will revert back to the Fish and Wildlife Service. Today, the Fish and Wildlife Service owns it—and the fifty acres and shoreline.

BUILDING CAROVA BEACH

Today's Carova Beach area is home to many millions of dollars in vacation rental homes and is no doubt visited annually by hundreds of thousands of tourists who provide an economic stimulus in the region that would have been hard to imagine only a few decades before. As the very first whiffs of business development began to materialize, this vacation landscape had to be literally carved out of the ocean and sand, not unlike Las Vegas or

*Disney World. Of note, the linkage between the duck clubs and the first
births of oceanside tourism is important, as one kind of tourism gave birth
to another across the generations.*

I sold the 550 acres I had collected in the cattle business to Mr. George T.
McLean in 1962 and retained all the hunting and grazing rights. In the
process of developing Carova Beach, I developed eighty some lots out of
that 550 acres for him. His CEO in later years, after Mr. McLean had
passed away, called me and said he had an opportunity to sell it to the
federal government. He said I would have to terminate my rights if they
decided to develop the land. I told him I didn't have any problem with it.
They sold it to the federal government as part of the Currituck Refuge
property in about 2006.

The first subdivision of any of the Outer Banks portion of Currituck
County began in 1967. It became known as the Carova Beach subdivision,
with the name being the first four letters of Carolina and first two letters
of Virginia, of course. That subdivision took place on property that had
originally been a part of the Currituck Hunt Club whose clubhouse was
located on Knotts Island. It included an area of 3.5 miles long from the
Virginia–North Carolina line, south to the property line that divided the
Swan Island Hunt Club property from the Currituck Hunt Club property.

That property had been purchased by George McLean from Portsmouth
in 1954, I believe it included all the oceanfront and back to a certain depth
determined by physical surveys. Mr. McLean owned it from 1954 to 1967.
He was a mentor to me. He had a partner named Jim Culbreath who was
half owner with Mr. McLean in that land. In 1967, Jim Kabler and a group
of investors—the firm was known at that time as Kabler Realty—had offices
in Sandbridge in Virginia Beach. He had developed all of the Sandbridge
subdivision along with his father-in-law, Mr. Harvey Lindsey, who owned
the Harvey Lindsey Realty enterprise. They operated a lot of commercial
properties. He was Jim Kabler's father-in-law.

Along about that time, in 1966, Jim and his wife were divorced, and he
was no longer associated with Mr. Lindsey. He attracted another group of
investors, and they approached Jim Culbreath and purchased his portion
of the property. Then they approached Mr. McLean with the idea of
subdividing the property, and Mr. McLean agreed that he wouldn't oppose it
and would support it. I had just completed a waterfront construction job that
I had sub-bid for Mr. McLean in Virginia Beach at the Rudee Inlet site—an
inlet which provides access to the ocean from a marina development on the

interior. Mr. McLean and Wilbert McCann had formed a joint venture and jettied both sides of the inlet on the north and south side. I had completed a similar structure in Carolina Beach for the Corps of Engineers that same year, 1966, and Mr. McLean contacted me. I had known him for a long time, of course. He asked me if I would build that sand trap feature of the jetty system at Rudee Inlet and build it for him, and I did. I completed that thing along in March, and they had just begun surveying in the Carova Beach Subdivision. I would spend the weeks up in Virginia Beach in a motel while I was doing the Rudee Inlet project there and come home on the weekends to take care of my livestock. My father was doing whatever needed to be done during the week.

I started that job in November and finished it in March 1966. I came right back, and Mr. McLean asked me if I would take over the Carova Beach subdivision, supervise it and do the physical work on the ground, engineering, running grades and levels and installing the drainage system. Later on, we got into the canal system and I took all that over and dug all those canals. I finished it in 1972. It took five years doing this Carova Beach subdivision. Kabler Realty did the promotion, the advertising and the selling. They sold like gangbusters. At that time, they still had access to bring prospective buyers down the beach from Virginia. They had a fleet of Jeep Wagoneers running all day back and forth bringing in buyers. The salespeople would be driving right by while I had equipment and men grading roads and digging canals, clearing the lots. Mr. McLean, prior to that, owned the Whalehead Club. He bought it from the Ray Adams estate. That was his first involvement on the Outer Banks. Mr. McLean didn't do any development at the Whalehead Club. He just bought it and held it as an investment. He did operate or subbed the operation to a group who used it for a boys school at one time, although the school was just the clubhouse.

I had a crane that we used to dig the canals in Carova Beach. It weighed seventy tons. I transported it down the beach. The navy let me use a concrete pad at Dam Neck Gunnery School to assemble it. It was so large you couldn't pull it down the highway. We shipped it in on three tractor trailers and put it together and assembled it at Dam Neck and towed it down the beach and began construction of those canals at Carova Beach. I had thirty-two wheels and tires under that crane on that trailer and a bulldozer pulling it. I finished all that construction in 1972. It took five years to finish that up. The canals took three years, and all the rest of the subdivision took us two years. This all took place in 1968 before there were any regulations, and we basically

A crane working on development in Currituck's Outer Banks. *Photo courtesy of Larry Riggs.*

were filling wetlands, that's what it amounts to. I used to hunt ducks all in that area. The purpose was to give boat access along with filling wetlands. I'm don't think any of it would get approved now.

Oceanfront lots in Carova Beach in 1972 started at $8,500 in section one. Section two oceanfront lots sold for $8,500. They moved down to section five, which had a few lots on the ocean, and all of section nine. Those lots sold for $12,500. Canal lots started at $4,500. Lot sales were rolling right along until the interest rates increased in the 1970s. Whalehead almost went belly-up, but there was a lull when sales and construction was depressed, then it picked up again.

Then again in the mid-1980s, we had another stagnant period of building and development. I have to say development on the Outer Banks of Currituck County was poorly managed. I have to say that in all fairness. At that time, Currituck County didn't even have a building code and didn't have one until I became commissioner in 1976. The first motion I made to the board was that Currituck County adopt the state building code in its entirety. Prior to that time the county didn't require any bond of any kind—no performance bond, no maintenance bond or anything.

That was another motion I made shortly thereafter. In Corolla, we had a case where all of Corolla village was bonded by a piece of marshland back in the back that was worth right next to nothing at that time. The developers who were developing Corolla Village had purchased the Whalehead Club property and financially they didn't get beyond the Corolla Village subdivision. I'm not sure the number of lots, maybe eighty-five. Mr. McLean had, in the meantime, leased the Whalehead Club to the Atlantic Research people. They were contractors for the federal government who were developing a solid fuel rocket engine, and they were using the Whalehead Club and this area because it was so remote. They constructed all that launching pad and all that stuff down there and never had a successful launch but ate up all the taxpayer's money.

I also operated a business for the developers from 1967 until 1988. It was solid waste disposal for the developers in the three northern subdivisions, Swan Beach, North Swan Beach and Carova Beach. I received a landfill permit from the old North Carolina Department of Natural Resources and Community Development. They had an office in Washington, North Carolina, and I was granted a landfill permit. I operated that landfill in the area that was not subject to development on the very back area of Carova Beach in the residual property that was not going to be platted and subdivided. I operated that from about 1967 until 1984 or 1985, when the county went to solid waste collection. Then I contracted with Waste Management to transport all the waste from those three subdivisions down to Corolla, where I met a Waste Management truck and off-loaded that waste from those three subdivisions to the Waste Management truck.

As development proceeded, I also had a big job in making sure those new homes had the services they needed in such a remote area. For ten

Aerial shot along Currituck's Outer Banks. *Photo courtesy of Twiddy & Company.*

years, I transported all the solid waste from Swan Beach, North Swan Beach and Carova Beach down to Corolla. I had a verbal contract. I've never had a written contract with anybody. I've done everything right off the top of my head with people. I did that for ten years. I started with Service Disposal, who were the first people who contracted with Currituck County for solid waste disposal. I did that for them for only six or eight months. Service Disposal sold their business to Waste Management and the president of Service Disposal, Mike Dobson, joined Waste Management as a vice president. I transported all that trash, waste, solid waste to Corolla twice a week in those eight-cubic-yard containers, and I compacted those things on site up there with a backhoe. The trucks I would meet in Corolla, in Whalehead, in one of those public parking lots. Met the front loader truck, they called it. They would pick those containers up and put them in their big compactor truck. I transported four of them at a time. Those things average 5,500 pounds each—ten tons I pulled all the time. My dad used to say he would see me go by with the truck and trailer load and wondered how in the world I did it. He said he bet if it was a wheelbarrow, I would put raise boards on it, because I overloaded everything. I had big 460-cubic-inch motors in these trucks, and they wouldn't last long. I had Allison transmissions and transfer cases and Dana differentials in them all, but it was only a three-quarter-ton truck.

ELECTRIC AND TELEPHONE SERVICE ON THE BEACHES

It's hard to imagine today, but the Currituck Outer Banks remained remarkably isolated and remote right up until the mid-1970s. We tend to think of small, isolated pockets in America only until World War II, yet there weren't many electric lights in Corolla even after the moon landing. In the many steps leading to what the place has become today, the arrival of public utilities marked the opportunity for private developers to have what had for almost a half century been available only to the Coast Guard stations—telephones and power.

Electricity came to Carova Beach in 1967 and telephone didn't come until 1974, I think. They had telephones and electricity in Corolla before that time. Initially, they ran the telephone on the same poles as the electricity. The original electricity for Carova Beach and North Swan Beach came from

Border between Virginia and Currituck's Outer Banks. *Photo courtesy of Edward Ponton.*

Virginia. Swan Beach and Seagull got their current from the Corolla area at about the same time. Then later on, Dominion Power North Carolina elected to get out of the Dominion Electric Virginia participation, so they put in that underground line that connected Swan Beach to North Swan Beach, and that eliminated the service from Virginia. Now False Cape Park is serviced by North Carolina. The Carolina service ends right there but it continues right on up into Virginia as Virginia service.

THE FIGHT FOR PUBLIC ACCESS AND TRANSPORTATION DEVELOPMENT

For many years, vehicle access to the Corolla area and farther north through North Carolina was problematic for the general public, as there was so little public infrastructure leading up to Currituck from Dare County in terms of paved roads. For both locals and visitors alike, this lack of access manifested itself for some time in a private gated access point just to the north of where the Sanderling Resort is to this day. The fight for that access, and the development it unleashed, is an inflection point in the history of tourism on the Currituck Outer Banks.

Along the modern Currituck Outer Banks, a Mr. Earl Slick of Winston-Salem played a key part as another large landowner and avid waterfowl enthusiast. For many years, the Slick family owned very large tracts of oceanfront land that today are called Pine Island. The family retains significant holdings and are noted, among many things, for their long-standing support to the National Audubon Sanctuary south of Corolla.

When I was first elected to the board of commissioners in 1976, Mr. Earl Slick still had his gate up across the road down there at Pine Island. Only people who owned property at that time were allowed to come through that gate. The gate was just north of Sanderling Inn, right in the sharp curve. If you notice when you come through there some time, there is a little wide place in the pavement. That is where that guardhouse sat.

If you'd drive up to that guardhouse from the south, if you lived on the mainland or anywhere else, you could come up to that guardhouse and tell that guard that you are going to visit "my cousin" who lives up in Carova Beach. It would have to be arranged beforehand. The person you were going to visit would have to call the guardhouse and tell them someone from the mainland was coming to visit. Other folks resorted to putting an anchor and an old piece of net and some rope or something in the back of their pickup truck, because commercial fishermen were allowed to come through there without a permit. It took eight years to get public access through there. State senator Marc Basnight from Manteo worked on that some kind of hard, and we owe him a debt of gratitude.

I took my seat on the board in 1976. The first Monday night in December, I asked the board to adopt a resolution requesting the Department of Transportation to effect, by whatever means was necessary, public access to the Currituck Outer Banks. And it took eight years. In 1986, that gate came down. Mr. Slick got $1 million for that right-of-way, and we got the public access.

I said to folks right then that Currituck County probably has twenty-five miles of the best recreational beach in the state; at time we had 8,600 people in Currituck County. We had all these people on the Currituck mainland who couldn't get to their own beach. If they wanted to go to the beach for a weekend or for a Sunday or Saturday afternoon outing and take their children, they had to go to Virginia Beach or Dare County. Or they had to tell a lie at Mr. Slick's guardhouse. Earl Slick wouldn't back off

$1 million for that right-of-way no matter what. And whatever access we were going to have had to be paved to state specifications before the state would let anyone drive on it. To make it happen, the developers up here paved it. The developers paid for the pavement on a density ratio, meaning each developer's responsibility was determined by the number of lots in his subdivision. Ocean Sands and Carova Beach paid the most because they had the greatest density. From the Virginia line to Ocean Sands, that was the last subdivision at that time. It finally opened in 1986.

I remember the day Mr. Slick invited the board of commissioners and other people to come over to Pine Island for a festivity under a big tent—a cook out and all that stuff. He stood up there that day and said, "I'm going to transfer title to all this oceanfront to the Audubon Society." He said they will not invoke their tax-exempt status. They are going to continue to pay taxes on all this oceanfront in Pine Island. The very next year, Audubon took advantage of their tax-exempt status. He owed $15 million in federal taxes at that time.

He had sold a television station and a bunch of real estate in Winston-Salem and incurred a $15 million tax liability. The federal government gave him credit for $7.5 million because he donated that land to the Audubon Society. There was also a provision in there that after ten years, he could transfer other

A beach view of the border between Virginia and Currituck's Outer Banks.

property to the Audubon Society and take the oceanfront back. And he did that. He then transferred the west side of NC 12 to the Audubon Society and took the oceanfront and developed it all into what is today Pine Island. He can now take the west side of NC 12 and give them the marshland, which is west of the highland. He had that in the Planning Department of Currituck County. The Planning Department was approached by some people who were proposing to develop the west side of State Highway 12 in Pine Island when the time was right to transfer the property. Despite what was said, those folks took their exemption the first year.

THE CREATION OF THE CURRITUCK NATIONAL WILDLIFE REFUGE

The Department of Interior, and U.S. Fish and Wildlife Service more specifically, destroyed all the future of this Outer Banks from Corolla to the Virginia line when they purchased the Monkey Island Hunt Club and the Swan Island Hunt Club, which at one time included Swan Beach and North Swan Beach. Between the two beaches was eighteen thousand feet of oceanfront in that Swan Island Hunt Club Property, six thousand feet in Swan Beach and six thousand feet in North Swan Beach. Then there was a center third of oceanfront property, which was another six thousand feet—in essence, three equal divisions of the Swan Island property took place, each of them considered equal by the distance on the oceanfront that was allowed for each of them. The developers and owners did that.

The center one-third of the Swan Island property, the developers of Swan Beach and the developers of Carova Beach had gotten together and purchased that center third. This was in the 1970s. The owners had financed the property for them, and they were going to develop it in the same mode they had developed Swan Beach and Carova Beach and North Swan Beach. In the late 1970s, though, interest rates went sky high; 18 percent was the going rate for residential funding at that time. If you bought a house and had a mortgage on it, the interest rate was 18 percent at one time back in the 1970s. These folks had notes in the bank and were only paying 6 or 8 percent. The bank called them all in because the bank wanted to take advantage of that 18 percent. These people couldn't make the notes, so they had a default in payment. The original loaners who had sold it to them reclaimed the property.

Now, in reclaiming that property, the developers of the two subdivisions insisted on a dedication of a one-hundred-foot-wide easement between Swan Beach and North Swan Beach, and that exists today. Had that been the case in the Monkey Island Tract, we would have a one-hundred-foot easement from Corolla to the Virginia line. The Fish and Wildlife Service, in this instance down here, didn't do it. In the negotiation that went on up there, the negotiation didn't take place with the Fish and Wildlife Service. It took place between the developers and the original owners. And for the equity that they had paid into the thing, they insisted upon some benefit from it, and the benefit was the one-hundred-foot easement that would connect the two subdivisions. Not many people know that thing exists. I had the deed book and page number for a long time. Today, there is a forty-four-thousand-volt power line underground on that easement from Swan Beach to North Swan Beach.

That is another thing: The Fish and Wildlife's purpose in closing the Virginia portion of the Outer Banks access to North Carolina was simply to deter development of the Outer Banks of Currituck County. They had in their grandiose plan and long-term plan the purchase of all of the Outer Banks of Currituck County, down to the Dare County line, and they did it in Virginia. For example, the Fish and Wildlife Service had bought the old Princess Anne Hunt Club in 1938 and created what they called the Back Bay Wildlife Refuge. Then in 1974, they initiated the permit system. By 1975 or 1976, they entered into an agreement with the State of Virginia to purchase all the land between the Back Bay Wildlife Refuge and the Virginia–North Carolina line. The Department of Interior's Bureau of Outdoor Recreation participated to the extent of 50 percent of the cost of purchasing all that property, and the state of Virginia furnished the other 50 percent. So, in effect, Bureau of Outdoor Recreation and the State of Virginia owned the False Cape State Park down to mean low water because every parcel of land they bought on the oceanfront in the False Cape Park required that the owner sign a quitclaim deed down to the mean low water mark, just to cover their tracks. They wanted to be sure they were covered not only by state law but by the purchase they had made from the individual. There is no doubt in my mind and no question about it—the Fish and Wildlife intent was to deter the development this Outer Banks of Currituck County and eventually purchase all of it.

They have purchased now all of the Monkey Island tract and all of the Swan Island tract that was left, and they have purchased all of the Carova Beach residual property—all that was eventually planned as an estate

Soundside view of Currituck's Outer Banks. *Photo courtesy of Larry Riggs.*

development. All those live oak trees in the back there along Ocean Pearl Road, over two-hundred-year-old live oak trees, limbs spread as much as one hundred feet from one side to the other, that was originally a part of the Currituck Hunt Club that had its headquarters on Knotts Island. It is all Carova Beach now. Since Fish and Wildlife purchased it, they have called it part of the Currituck Outer Banks refuge system. They have combined the Swan Island property, the Currituck Club property and the Monkey Island property into what they call Currituck County National Wildlife Refuge. I know this sounds like criticism, but I think it's just the truth—Fish and Wildlife doesn't want any development. I call them empire builders. They want everything they own and everything that adjoins them. That was Lady Bird Johnson's thing, you know. She was buying all that land down on the Gulf Coast when Lyndon Johnson was president. Somebody asked her once if she wanted to own the whole world. She said no, she just wanted to own what she owned now and all that adjoins her. She bought up thousands and thousands of acres of land and established a huge network of radio and television stations in those years.

POLITICS AT THE TIME

As Mr. Ernie watched the development of the Currituck Outer Banks, it was only a matter of time until he decided to run for office. It's important to note here that separation of Currituck County, mentioned earlier as having a "beach" side and a "mainland" side, that for years has separated residents in both body and philosophy in some cases. Mr. Ernie's elected offices would always be associated with the beach.

County Commissioner

Backing up just a bit, by 1974, I was concerned about what was happening in the county in the way of development. I saw it on the mainland too. Harold Capps was a commissioner on the county board of commissioners at that time, elected from Fruitville Township. He had been on the board for twenty-one years. He was appointed to the board when Norwood Ansell was elected to the general assembly from Knotts Island, and Harold was appointed to complete that term, then he won elections after that. So, Harold said he was not going to be a candidate for reelection. I went to Knotts Island and sat down with him one day and asked him if that was the case, and he said, "No, I'm not going to be a candidate." I told him I was going to begin attending county commissioner's meetings. I told him I thought I might be a candidate in his stead if he wasn't going to run. He said he was not going to run. I attended every county commission meeting from then until I was elected, and I felt I had a pretty good feeling for what was going on by that time.

That was the only time in the history of North Carolina when Democratic primaries were held in August rather than in May. It turns out both Harold and Norwood Ansell filed for that seat, and I beat them both in the primary in August. I was elected in the general election because I didn't have any Republican opposition. I don't believe you could have found a person that would admit that he was a Republican in Currituck County in those days, anywhere. Anyway, I didn't have any opposition.

When I took my seat the first Monday in December, I offered a motion to the board of commissioners that we adopt the state building code in its entirety, and we also should require any improvements in place before final plat approval would be granted for any subdivision. Prior to that time, the development of Corolla Village was a classic example; the developers had done this subdivision, First Street, Second Street and Third Street, they were called in those days, although they have been renamed since then. No one had a plan for the maintenance or improvements of those streets or roads, except to bulldoze the bushes out of the way and name them.

The county required what wasn't really a performance bond or maintenance bond, didn't really have a name for it. Rather than put up any cash money, they gave the county a deed of trust on that property and marshland back in the back, which is today the Lighthouse Club. The county valued it at $35,000, and that was estimated to be the cost of constructing First, Second and Third Streets. Well, it lay back there for years, and that took place all over this county. Anybody on the Currituck County mainland who did a subdivision, all he had to do was give the county a deed to four or five acres of swamp, marsh, and he could walk away from it. If he didn't do the roads, didn't do what he agreed to do, all the county had was four or five acres of marsh or swamp and nothing you could do with it. We had several subdivisions on the mainland the same way. I fought those things for I don't know how many years until finally we got them done, although we never did get them done in Corolla. I'm still getting letters from a man in New Jersey about what was Second Street at that time, now Schoolhouse Lane on the ocean side of the street. He sent me more literature for ten or fifteen years now. He said there was supposed to be $35,000 somewhere, and he wants someone to fix Second Street or Schoolhouse Lane with it. He went so far as to find the $35,000. It's in an escrow fund at Billy Brumsey's law office, and it's still there. No one has ever used it. That $35,000 wouldn't do much today.

Anyway, I was upset about things like that that were going on around the county, so that is why I ran for commissioner. I was elected in 1976. The second meeting I proposed the state building code, and it was approved

Beaches along Currituck's Outer Banks. *Photo courtesy of Edward Ponton.*

and went into effect in February 1977. There didn't appear to be any opposition to this, but they didn't reelect me four years later either. What that thing did was stop all these subdivisions on the Currituck Outer Banks. When we required all improvements to be in place before final plat approval and that all streets and roads be built to state specifications, that stopped all the subdivisions on the Outer Banks. It worked the same on the mainland. That was my object—to get the mainland—but I got the beach too without realizing it. But it was a good thing. It needed to stop. We had 3,300 lots from Corolla to the North Carolina–Virginia line without any provision at all for maintenance of the roads and streets and no provision for drainage systems, no provision for public utilities—no nothing. Absolutely nothing.

A NEW KIND OF LOCAL POLITICS

As I ran for office and worked with taxpayer money, one thing I did was go door to door. Nobody had ever done that before. I would drive down the Currituck mainland from the Virginia line to Point Harbor. I'll give you an example. I stopped one day when I saw a lady on a ladder in front of her house—a small little farmhouse right along the highway. I stopped, got out of my car and went over to her. She was up on that ladder painting the front of her house. I said, "I know you want an excuse to get down off that ladder and drink a glass of iced tea or something." She said, "I sure do." And that's the kind of rapport I developed with people in this county. I related to people in my district more than anybody ever had before.

By moving to adopt the state building code in its entirety and to require all improvements in place before final plat approval, I was taking on some of the "big wheels" on the mainland. For example, a Mr. Gray owned Bells Island. He was publisher of the *Saturday Evening Post* and owned the Curtis Publishing Company. Jerry Hardesty was a member of the three-member planning commission, such as it was back in those days, and he was also the county extension agent, who was a kind of go-between between the North Carolina State University and the farm community in the county. Mr. Gray took a liking to Jerry Hardesty. Mr. Gray had become advanced in years and didn't much participate at Bells Island any longer. He had a nice black Angus cattle herd over there—purebred herd. He had a herdsman named Slim Williams who had been separated from the service here after World War II and was a really good herdsman, originally from Texas. After Mr. Gray became advanced in years, he just decided to disburse the herd. He did, and that was in the late '50s. This friend of mine from Deep Creek bought several brood cows out of that herd. Jerry got close to Mr. Gray, and Mr. Gray told him he was going to sell but said he didn't want this island developed. It was primarily a duck hunting club, had a lot of duck blinds in the marshes and along the shores. It was a very modest club. The clubhouse itself was a small building, about two or three small bedrooms, but he had an extremely nice barn and corrals and concrete feeding troughs in place. That still exists on Bells Island today.

Johnny Messina bought that part of Bells Island and retained it and kept a few horses there and a few cows. Needless to say, when I stepped on some of those big toes, it got me defeated in my reelection bid. I thought we did a lot of good things between 1976 and 1980.

Two years later, in 1982, I announced my candidacy for the at-large seat, along with Wilson Snowden. Baxter Williams was the incumbent. In the primary, Wilson got the most votes, Baxter got the next most votes and I came in third, but I don't think between Wilson and I were more than 100 to 125 votes difference. After the primary election that night, a radio station called me from Elizabeth City, I think. They wanted to know what I was going to do about the primary runoff because there could be one. I said if Baxter Williams called for a runoff, I'm going to support Wilson. As a result of that, Baxter decided not to call for a runoff, and Wilson became the at-large commissioner then. I won the election in 1984, lost again in 1988, won again in 1992 and served from 1992 until 2008. I think another thing I did that reflected on my service was I, very early on, when I was first elected to the board of commissioners, I used to conduct what I called local government meetings in my district, Knotts Island and in Corolla, which was in the Poplar Branch Township, of course, but I held them in Corolla as well.

I would invite all of the county commissioners to attend that meeting and all the major staff people. The register of deeds, the tax supervisor, the director of planning and inspections or whomever. We took questions from the public and explained to them current endeavors that were being considered for growth in the county. I did those meetings about once every two months. I never had another commissioner within his township do it until the election of 1994, I guess. Paul O'Neal, who was elected from Poplar Branch Township, initiated two or three, what they called them, town meetings here in Corolla at the fire station. I thought that was a very productive thing to do, and I gained a lot of information from those meetings. By and large, they were well attended in every case at Knotts Island and those meetings at Carova Beach at the fire station. At all those meetings there would be some civic group. The Women's Auxiliary of the Knotts Island Fire Department would always furnish refreshments, coffee, soft drinks, cookies, sandwiches, cake and things like that at the school over there. We would have a little intermission about halfway through the meeting, and folks would take that opportunity to talk among themselves in

A piece of driftwood on Currituck's Outer Banks. *Photo courtesy of Larry Riggs.*

a different environment other than in the meeting itself and discuss what we had been discussing up to that point. Then there was always a summary after the question-and-answer session was over. We would summarize what we had talked about, and if there were some questions that came up for which none of us had an answer, we certainly made note of it and resolved that question in the coming week or days and got back to whoever had asked the question. I thought they were very productive and I hope stay in place far into the future.

Trying to Bridge the Divides—County Redistricting

I had a battle over redistricting. The first time it came up, the board didn't want to agree with me. I thought that every part of this county that was not contiguous to the mainland should be in the same district. That is all of the Outer Banks, all of Knotts Island and all of Gibbs Woods. Those are three areas in this county that are not contiguous to the mainland. I thought they all had the same needs, and we could address them all in one fashion.

They wanted to put Bells Island in this district and wanted to keep half of the Outer Banks. They wanted to keep all of Pine Island and Monteray Shores, I suppose, in Poplar Branch Township, and then put this part in district one up there with Knotts Island and put Gibbs Woods in another district with Bells Island and the Tulls Creek area. I thought that was a foolish thing to do, and I wondered why they were doing it.

And it came to my realization that, well, let's just say it had a lot to do with who was going to run for office from what district. In short, we put all of the Outer Banks in district one, all of Knotts Island and all of Gibbs Woods. That's how it is today. There is some good and some bad about it.

I took a terrible tongue lashing around the county for opposing unification, they called it, or incorporation of the entire county. I didn't think that was right. I thought it was something to prohibit the people over on the Outer Banks if they were to decide to incorporate and could justify incorporation here; it would have prohibited them from doing that if the entire county became a town. You couldn't create another town within a town. That was their whole purpose, to defeat any possibility of Corolla and this lower area of the Outer Banks from incorporating. There are no incorporated municipalities in Currituck County. A lot of people don't know that there are only three counties in North Carolina, three out of one hundred, without a town—Camden, Currituck and Hyde. Hyde did incorporate Engelhard one time, but it didn't last long, and they had to be unincorporated, if that is a word.

AND JUST SHAREABLY GOOD STORIES

Some of Mr. Ernie's memories just make for good storytelling over dinner and are too good not to be shared. His battles with the federal government over his access through Virginia are the stuff of local legend and add yet another remarkable chapter to his varied and fiercely independent streak.

How to See a Big Storm Coming

The very first thing I start to look for is—and I learned this from my dad—if the wind is northeast and the ocean gets rough, you look real closely to see if the current is going north, against the wind. We call it a crossbow. If you see that, it is usually the very beginning of a circular action somewhere that is affecting us this far away.

The Beached Whale

The county called me one day when I wasn't on the board and said, "Ernie, there is a big whale washed up on the beach over there, and we need to dispose of it. Can you get rid of it?" I told them I'd go look and call them back. That whale was seventy feet long laying there in the surf. I came back and called the county manager and told him I would get rid of it. I had a

Beached whale on Currituck's Outer Banks. *Photo courtesy of Edward Ponton.*

great big four-wheel-drive loader with diesel in it and three guys working with me. I bought three more bush hooks, already had two or three. I put a generator in the back of my truck with a sharpening machine. I kept one man sharpening those bush hooks. It took twenty minutes to cut up that whale, and those hooks would be so dull they wouldn't cut it. I had that big loader hooked up to that whale. It was low water. I had a great big towing hawser that tugboats used to tow barges with. We had put it around that thing's tail and tied it to the front-end loader. We would sit there, and every time a wave would come, we would rev that motor and pull on that thing to move it a little closer to the beach. I told the boys to keep pulling on him, try to get him in so we could still work on him at high water, and he won't be submerged. There was a terrible odor coming from that whale, and the wind was blowing right toward the loader. The man I had operating the loader called me over and said he couldn't stay there any longer; he couldn't stand the odor. So, I told him I would handle the loader. I got up on that loader and had it running wide open. There were vehicles coming by—people taking pictures and all that stuff.

At one point, a Jeep stopped right beside that loader, and a guy got out and walked over and was talking to me. I couldn't understand what he was saying from the motor making so much noise, so I locked the brake on the loader and shut the motor off. I asked him to repeat his question, and he said, "What did you use for bait?" I was dumbfounded when he asked me that question. That Jeep had Pennsylvania plates, and I love that story.

We cut that whale up and got about two-thirds of it buried. I had a crane at the time, and we took the crane over there and picked up the last third of it. I have pictures of that crane holding the last third of that whale up in the air before we buried it. I'm sure I got paid for that. I guess I've taken care of five or six whales for the county at different times. The Smithsonian Institute and Virginia Institute of Marine Science had something to do with some. I got to know a man from the Smithsonian Institute who came down to do some physical examination of all these carcasses. Someone would call him. He told me that that particular species of whale weighed one ton to the foot. Seventy feet long, and it weighed seventy tons.

THE GHOST OF WASH WOODS STATION

The Wash Woods Station has, in its local history, a reputation for a residing ghost named Mose who, while friendly in nature, has more than one well-known local telling stories of their own encounter.

We had a Coast Guardsman who was stationed there nicknamed Mose. His father, Walter Williams, was the first commanding officer of the new Wash Woods Coast Guard Station in 1918. Walter's son was Raymond Williams—our Mose. He enlisted in the Coast Guard and spent almost his entire twenty years right there at Wash Woods. He didn't die in the line of duty, though, as some have suggested. He retired from the Coast Guard,

Wash Woods Station. *Photo courtesy of Doug Twiddy.*

bought a little farm over on Knotts Island and lived there when he died. He married one of Mr. Leon White's daughters of the L.R. White estate. Mr. Leon had eleven children; one of them died in World War II. Ross was the oldest, and I think there were three sons and eight daughters in his family.

How I Got Into the Horse Business

The Coast Guard initiated what they called a horse patrol during World War II. The United States Cavalry became mechanized when World War II started. They had all these cavalry horses all over the country. Front Royal, Virginia, was a large remount station, they called it, and they brought remount horses from the West there by railroad cars. They had a large facility in there that trained those horses, broke them for cavalry use, and the older horses went somewhere else.

The Coast Guard took a bunch of those horses and stationed them at every station. Wash Woods Coast Guard Station had a full complement when the war began. There were eight men at Wash Woods then. Mr. Pell Austin became the officer in charge of the Wash Woods Coast Guard Station in 1941. They built stables, temporary ones, at all these Coast Guard stations, and they brought eight or ten or maybe a dozen of the cavalry horses to each station. New recruits were assigned those stations to patrol the beaches. No vehicular traffic was allowed on the beach after sundown in the afternoon, nor before daylight the next morning. You couldn't drive a vehicle on that beach if you were fortunate enough to even have one.

The Currituck Beach Coast Guard Station built some stables just west of the station, and they had eight or ten horses there. They used the lighthouse keeper's house to store hay. That building was full of hay. The Wash Woods Station used some of the hay from there. They would bring it over by barge from the mainland and store it in all those rooms of the lighthouse keeper's house during this horse patrol.

When the war was over, the Coast Guard was selling these horses. They were holding auctions at a place known as Princess Anne Country Club, in this area, up in Virginia Beach. Now this same thing went on all up and down the coast. Long Island, New York, had this horse patrol, Fire Island Inlet Coast Guard Station on up to and across to Montauk Point and on down to Jones Beach and all those places had Coast Guard Stations, and the same horse patrol operated there.

In this area, they took those horses to Princess Anne Country Club, up near the Cavalier Hotel, which had a large equestrian facility and held a public auction. A lot of people bought them. All those cavalry horses had a brand beneath their mane. They didn't brand them where it was visible. You had to lift their mane to find the brand. Some of the horses were purchased by people in the area. Raymond Williams, for example, was stationed at the Wash Woods Coast Guard Station, and he bought a black gelding that was a cavalry horse, about a five or six-year-old horse, a good substantial horse, weighed about 1,000 or 1,100 pounds. Raymond stayed at that Coast Guard station for a couple years after World War II, and he used that horse.

His father-in-law was Leon White. L.R. White and their family still own about 450 acres of land up behind Swan Beach. Mr. Leon's middle son, Columbus, still had a little bit of livestock on this beach, and Raymond tended to his livestock for him. Columbus moved away at the beginning of World War II, but he still had a few cattle that stayed here during the war. Raymond retired from the Coast Guard and moved to Knotts Island. He had in the meantime bought a small farm over there, and his wife and small children were over there. I bought that black gelding from him and

A wild horse on Currituck's Outer Banks. *Photo courtesy of Edward Ponton.*

kept him until he died. I don't remember, he was probably in his early twenties when he finally died of old age. There were two other horses here. One was a horse named Major. That was his name as far as the cavalry was concerned and branded under his mane on his neck. He was a quarter horse with a stripe on his face and four white stockings. A fellow by the name of Gray bought him, and when he moved back to Hatteras, I bought that horse from him.

I had a few horses like these, a couple quarter horses and Appaloosas, that I was breeding. I had leased 3,000 acres from the Swan Island Hunt Club. Everything from the Currituck Hunt Club property down to the Swan Beach property. I owned the 550 acres that was an integral part of the Swan Island property. That was where I was running cattle. I had 11 miles of fence that I built that essentially fenced in that marshland. My corrals were up near the Wash Woods Station where my dad and I were living then—sometime around 1950. My father had a sorrel gelding that I had given him, gave him the same name of the horse we owned when I was a child, Sonny Boy. That was what Dad always called him. That was a foal out of one of my mares, and my dad liked it. We gelded it, and he used it for as long as the horse lived, helping me with the cattle. My uncle still had a cattle herd, and he had a bad knee and didn't ride horses much in his later years, so he depended on us to get his cattle up for him too. My dad and I would do that, and I had these other horses.

The Pine Island Club and Horses

A Dr. Baum bought the Pine Island Club for its value as a grazing land and the marshes and for the hunting value. The oceanfront didn't mean anything at all to him—nothing. He had a little band of horses down there, and Mr. Lloyd O'Neal bought this colt from him, grew it out and called it Bob. After we would get through the cattle—usually started in early June until about September—we were herding up cattle or sheep two or three times a month. Mr. Lloyd would finish in the fall with all that stock, would take that horse up the beach where there was some grazing, up in the area behind the Wash Wood Coast Guard Station today, that was all marshland, but a lot of Bermuda grass and a lot of brown top millet and a lot of saltmarsh grass. A lot of the livestock grazed that area for years.

Mr. Lloyd would just take him up there and turn him loose. The old horse would winter up there on his own, and in the spring, Mr. Lloyd would go back up there with an old ragged pick-up truck. Mr. Lloyd owned a hunt club right there next to Penny's Hill. He would go back up there in the spring with an old metal bucket with a little bit of corn. He could see the horse out there in the marsh. He would call him a few times and shake the bucket of corn, and the horse would come right out to him. Mr. Lloyd would put a rope around his neck, tie him to the back of the pick-up truck and drive slowly all the way home. The horse would follow right behind him. He would keep him home all summer. It was a different time

CAPTAIN BILL BOWDEN AND THE "RUMRUNNER DETAIL"

Sol Sanderlin's [recall Mr. Sanderlin from Corolla Village] son Sidney was on the rumrunner detail with my father at Fort Pierce, Florida, during Prohibition in 1929. They captured a rumrunner boat that was coming in from the Bahamas or somewhere with a load of whiskey. When they intercepted that boat, they would tow that rumrunner back to Fort Pierce to the Coast Guard base. One of the guys that was on the rumrunner boat—nobody searched them or anything—was the warrant officer, and my dad was the chief mate on the boat. Dad was down in the aft cockpit. Those picket boats had two cockpits, one up forward and one back aft. The engine room was in between. My dad was in the aft cockpit with part of the crew. Sidney Sanderlin had one of the crew up in the wheelhouse with him. The guy that he had with him had a gun, and he shot Sidney Sanderlin right in the back of the head and killed him. They had a public hanging and built a scaffolding right in town square in Fort Pierce, Florida, and hanged the guy. As ironic as it may seem, in 1940, Uncle Sol's grandson accidentally shot me with a pistol. The bullet struck me right there in my hip bone and traveled through my intestines. Damn near killed me. That was in 1940 on Armistice Day. His father was killed in my Dad's presence, and then he had the misfortune to have a gun go off accidentally and almost killed me.

MY RIGHTS, MY ROADS AND
MY TRANSPORTATION BATTLE

The Department of Interior purchased, in 1938, a hunt club in Virginia that was known as the Princess Anne Hunt Club. There were 3.5 miles of oceanfront, and they purchased everything from the ocean to Back Bay. Those of us who lived on the Outer Banks, certainly from the village of Corolla and north, were economically and socially oriented to that area of lower Virginia Beach or Princess Anne County, as it was known as for many years. We had a Roses there, so we shopped there, we banked there and some went to church there in Virginia, who were closer than the little church in Corolla.

The Department of Interior did not object to the vehicular traffic that was necessary for us to move back and forth over that tidal beach area. We enjoyed a very good relationship with the Department of Interior over those years. After World War II, people had some money and leisure time and would travel on that beach with all kinds of vehicles. Going south, getting away from the populated areas, most of them just joy riding on weekends and spending overnight camping trips as far down as Corolla. Most of that activity took place up on the isolated areas of that beach, which are now Swan Beach and Carova Beach. The Department of Interior, in 1970, three years after the first subdivision of the Outer Banks in Currituck County began, decided that this vehicular traffic was "detrimental to the purposes that the refuge was established." I have heard that phrase so many times I have it memorized.

Back in 1954, the federal government had deeded to the State of Virginia a fifty-five-foot easement through the Back Bay Wildlife Refuge for the purpose of constructing an all-weather road to connect Princess Anne County in Virginia with Currituck County in North Carolina. Long story short, Virginia chose to void that deed in North Carolina somehow. That was the first thing the Department of Interior did to control the traffic. Then they exercised their right of ownership to eliminate vehicular traffic on the tidal beach area by virtue of the fact they owned the beach area down to the mean low water. That went through a process of litigation for about four years.

The developers were attempting to maintain that route of travel in order to get to the subdivisions they were creating in North Carolina. That was in court from 1969 or 1970 and terminated in 1974. The decision of the Fourth Circuit Court of Appeals brought the Department of

Interior to initiate a permit system in 1974. The permit system initially accommodated anyone who owned improved property in what became the False Cape State Park and abutted the refuge and the North Carolina line on the south. Those people were allowed a permit to travel on the beach. Residents of the Currituck Outer Banks were given permits, but no provision was made initially to accommodate commercial enterprises, and I, at that time, had a commercial construction operation going on supporting those subdivisions.

The commercial fisherman objected to the rules because they were not accommodated with a permit that allowed them to transport fish to markets in Virginia. During the process of developing the regulations in 1974, there were a number of public hearings held in Virginia Beach. It was there that the commercial fishermen noted their opposition to the proposed rules that would not allow them a permit. Finally, the Department of Interior relented and did allow the commercial fishermen and five employees to be included in the permit system that was adopted in 1974. But I was the only non-fisherman to get a permit. I was classified as a livestock farmer and a contractor.

My controversy with the U.S. Fish and Wildlife Service started because they told me, as a commercial contractor, they would not accommodate me. They refused to give me a permit for my employees. My position was I certainly should be accommodated as the commercial fishermen had. I took offense to it and continued to transport materials and employees through the refuge to whatever projects I had going on. I had completed all the canal system in the Carova Beach subdivision in 1972, before the rules were adopted by Fish and Wildlife Service. I kept some of those employees to help install foundation pilings for cottages, clearing lots and site prep.

I don't remember the years, but for about five years, they had me in and out of federal court, charging me with trespassing. I managed to be acquitted in four of those criminal charges of trespass. I don't know if it was good or bad, but I chose to represent myself each time I had to appear in Federal District Court, and I managed to win those first four. In one of those cases, the Fish and Wildlife Service had failed to renew its regulations in a timely manner. I did research and so forth, and I learned they had elapsed on January 1, and they had me in court again in February or March charged with trespassing. I noted to the judge that the regulations were not even valid because they had expired. That was one technicality in which I won acquittal.

It finally got down to the last time I went to court, and somebody said, "Ernie, just get a lawyer." So, I did, and I got convicted.

The judge sentenced me to ten days in jail. I knew the sheriff of Virginia Beach, and he had the report down there that I had to serve the ten days. He got in touch with me and said, "Ernie, we don't discharge anybody on weekends here. If you'll show up on Sunday afternoon—" Well, anyway, I only had to serve five days. Fish and Wildlife decided to go one step further and cited me again. I had noted an objection every time I had appeared before the federal judge that they would not allow me a jury trial.

I cited the Sixth Amendment to the Constitution, which clearly states that every individual shall be entitled to a trial by jury, whether it is a criminal or civil charge, and no matter how menial the charge, misdemeanor or felony. The federal government takes the position that unless you are charged with a felony or a crime that carries a sentence of more than one year in prison or more than $10,000 fine, you won't get a jury trial. You have to be charged with a felony or have to be charged with a violation which carries a penalty of more than one year in jail or more than a $10,000 fine. That was really the thing that kept me so adamantly opposed to what they were doing. They had never really offered any compromise. I told them I would never accept any permit that required a fee, and the first permit they put out they charged everybody $90 a year. I guess that is what ticked them off, because I wouldn't even make application for the permit to begin with, because they were going to charge $90. Every person, without exception, who got a permit that first go-round paid that $90, including my father.

I wouldn't pay it, or even make application for it, so I guess it was like Black Gum against Thunder. Anyway, the final time I went to court, Judge J. Calvitt Clarke, the federal judge, sentenced me to fifty-five days of jail, based on the number of violations. I had 110 violations, and he was going to convict me of 55 of them that day. I'll never forget him. He sat there shaking his finger at me and he said, "Mr. Bowden, I've got fifty-five more days waiting for you." And he sent me up to James City County to serve that fifty-five days. You don't get any good behavior time for a federal sentence, so I served my fifty-five days there. I came back and did the same thing I'd been doing all along. Finally, they called me and wanted me to meet with the Fish and Wildlife attorney. They wanted me to meet them at their headquarters on Virginia Beach Boulevard and discuss my travel situation. As a result of that meeting, they gave me a commercial permit and allowed me five employees, and by then, they had eliminated the fee. They only charged the ninety dollars for that first year. I've enjoyed that privilege. They say it's not a right, but I think it's a right that I have, based my defense on the very fact that for generations people of the Currituck

Aerial shot of homes along Currituck's Outer Banks. *Photo courtesy of Larry Riggs.*

Outer Banks have utilized that area for that various reasons that I stated all along. A lot of our families have moved up to the Tidewater area, and I felt that it was a right that people had earned.

Judge McKinzie, who approved the rules that the Department of Interior finally accepted, stated that those longtime residents of the Currituck Outer Banks had established certain inalienable rights, which the Department of Interior must address in developing their rules and regulations. That is what allowed those few of us who did qualify for permits to acquire them.

While all of this was going on, I was reelected to the board of commissioners in the election of November 1983, and I went back on the board the first Monday of December 1983. And I had to go to court on January 5, 1984. That is when Judge Clark convicted me and sent me to jail for fifty-five days. After I got out of jail, I got the permit in 1984. I was a commissioner while I was in jail. The chairman would bring the minutes of the meetings up to me in James City County Jail in Virginia. The judge sent me as far away as he could get me. He wanted it to be as inconvenient for people to visit me as he could make it.

CONCLUSION

These memories have captured, in some small way, a glimpse of the way things were from a time rapidly disappearing, like a footprint in the sand, from our memory.

In modern times, so much of our history becomes an algorithm on the internet, yet we know that the place today is as much a reflection of the turn of the twentieth century as it is the twenty-first. As the Currituck Outer Banks continues its winding path of commercial development and natural conservation, Mr. Ernie shares a few thoughts about the future and some of the challenges the next generation will inherit.

It is perhaps widely agreed upon that the potential for the long-discussed Mid-Currituck Bridge to finally link the Currituck Outer Banks to not only the mainland but also the larger world is the best economic catalyst the county may ever see. As with all developments at this scale, however, the idea of the bridge itself has become a fault line between the commercial interests of change and those who worry, like the poet, that we will lose what we had in the pursuit of not getting what we wanted.

For those who might not have visited the area, it's worth noting that there remains only one north–south road leading to the Currituck Outer Banks. In the summer vacation season, the road is congested with industry and visitors, contributing to a longer-standing debate on capacity, safety and quality of life.

A sound-side view of Currituck's Outer Banks. *Photo courtesy of Larry Riggs.*

THE DIVIDE BETWEEN THE MAINLAND AND THE CURRITUCK OUTER BANKS

The divide between the Banks and the mainland is terrible, although that has always been the case. Of course, for many years, there wasn't anyone on the beach to be one way or another. At one time, the federal government was proposing to buy all of this Banks, and they wanted the blessing of the Board of Commissioners of Currituck County. I think they said $15 million. This was before all this development had gotten off the ground. It was taking place but hadn't really progressed too far. People were interviewed on the Currituck County mainland. People there were saying yes, they thought the federal government should take it, because it would cost the county a lot of money if they let those people develop it over there. That was the attitude, kind of us and them.

As I said earlier, in those early years there weren't enough people over on this beach to make much difference. This us and them thing, syndrome or whatever you choose to call it, came up primarily after World War II and up into the 1950s and 1960s when people began to return to the beach with a certain education they had gotten somewhere else. Having lived away during the war, they were introduced to a lot of things they had never heard of in their early life, so they found their voice, I guess, and began to talk a little. Then this thing developed us and them. That was a thing of mine from day one, was to try to put this county together as one entity. I said, "I know we can't do it physically or geographically, but damned if we can't do it in a manner that will let us all live together and work together for

Beaches of Currituck's Outer Banks. *Photo courtesy of Larry Riggs.*

a common cause." It never got any further than that, as hard as I worked on that thing for all those years. It has never seemed to make any progress. I would think I was doing something, holding these little local government meetings and bringing members from the county mainland, members in government and local civic organizations and things, cohabitation, try to get the people together to talk about common interests. I would think I was doing something, and all of a sudden, it didn't take but one person from over there to talk to a reporter, and it would knock it all to hell. That guy would have something to say just because he had a reporter's attention, had his ear for a minute or two, and of course, the reporter wasn't looking for the right person to talk with, and things would just go back ten years when that article would get published.

TOWARD THE FUTURE: A MID-CURRITUCK BRIDGE TO THE NORTHERN BEACHES

As traffic numbers continue to grow, I don't think people down south realize how much the bridge will impact their traffic bottlenecks—as I've long said, the Currituck Outer Banks has twenty-five miles of the best beaches in the country. If the bridge comes through, traffic down south will be reduced greatly, and many more people will opt to visit our area and not Hatteras Island or even Ocracoke. We'll be discovered again. And that leads to more problems, too—we had better do a better job of planning than we did during the last several booms for sure.

On these northern beaches, frankly, I don't know that these beaches can stand a whole lot more than we are seeing today in their present condition. There's got to be some changes made up here to accommodate any increase or influx of permanent residency. There has got to be something done between day users and vehicular traffic. [Since this session, the county has instituted a permit process for beach access in the summer months.] We've had about five fatalities related to motor vehicles in the last seven years up here. I don't know how much impact this area can stand in terms of the traffic and conflict between day users and residents.

THE IMPACTS OF DEVELOPMENT

My father was eighty-four when he died, so Dad saw some of it changing here, and he had mixed emotions. First of all, I think he was concerned about what was actually happening to the land physically. We had lived here all those years with the land in its natural state. We have far more drainage problems today than we did when I was growing up in these areas simply because—well I don't know prior to the Depression—but during the Depression, a lot of permanent drainage was constructed by those public works programs, such as the WPA, and the Civil Conservation Corps. Some of those drainage systems exist today, but not many of them are functional. Most of them have grown up and built over.

After the Depression, when the economy finally came back after World War II and folks had a little leisure and income, people could have an automobile, better housing and live a better lifestyle. We didn't have a drainage problem to speak of then. Most of those 1930s things were still in place. Nobody here had created a drainage problem.

Subdivisions have created drainage problems in that the configuration of the land has been changed. We have moved dunes into low areas, and those low areas were drainage areas at one time. But now we have filled those, and

The woods of Currituck's Outer Banks. *Photo courtesy of Larry Riggs.*

Currituck Beach Lighthouse. *Photo courtesy of Larry Riggs.*

in so doing, we have affected the drainage upstream, so to speak, up there, that that water by natural process just found its way to the sound or to the swamp, whatever was the case. The same problem exists on the mainland. Developers have irresponsibly filled existing drainage systems and submitted a drainage plan—every subdivision has to submit, along with its subdivision regulation request, a drainage plan to the soil and water conservation department. That plan is reviewed by them, and unfortunately, some of these drainage plans that have been devised by some developers just don't work. They impacted something that they shouldn't have been impacting and were eliminating something that was working before and doesn't work any longer. I have farmers tell me on the mainland that in lots of cases they can't get over land with a combine or tractor to farm it, that they used to get over with no problem at all. If they have, not an extreme rainy season, but more than usual rainy time, they have to wait until land dries up some before they can farm that very field, because downstream, someone had filled a ditch and cut a new ditch that didn't address the farm need back up here.

My dad would look at that like he did when he was still here and say, "I don't know what we're going to do about the mosquitos this year. Everything back there is going to pool up full of water." That's what Dad would say.

As of this writing, Mr. Ernie Bowden is ninety-five years young and is still a resident of the Currituck Outer Banks. He has become a wonder in many ways—a living link with a lost era and a lost place while losing none of his hesitation around speaking his truth without fear, and I suspect he would entirely reject the notion that he has become, in any way, a walking monument to a time gone by.

The ocean tribes of the postwar Outer Banks are fewer in their connections today as the world grows larger while many of the old landmarks—the old stations—have simply disappeared from view as developers and nature itself shape and reshape the lands of the Bowdens.

Monuments are, of course, for the living, and perhaps it is enough to say that there are few people, past or present, who knew the place and its people more deeply than the cattleman from Seagull. We are blessed for his tracks along the shore and fortunate that, through his memory, the ocean shall not reclaim them.

ACKNOWLEDGEMENTS

One only fails alone—success, on the other hand, comes only with the help of others. In this project, I remain deeply indebted from the outset to a group of people who believe the past is indeed worthy of telling. Michael Gary's work is the key to this history and all of the book is a direct reflection of his efforts. Pam Merrell, of Currituck County, painstakingly and patiently transcribed the oral histories into a working document, without which this book would not exist in this form. The distinguished Miles Daniels of Wanchese brought sunlight to the project with his vision for capturing the past, and without him the book would not be in your hands. Lastly, I thank my wife, Anna, and my two daughters, Elyse and Leah, for their patience as I whiled away the hours lost in thought in a small Hyde County home.

As for any errors or omissions in the storytelling, those are mine and mine alone. Mr. Ernie's memory is no doubt sharper than my ability to collect it.

ABOUT THE AUTHOR

Photo courtesy of Shane Moore.

Clark Twiddy is the president of Twiddy & Company, an asset management and hospitality firm founded in 1978 along the North Carolina Outer Banks. He was raised in Duck, North Carolina, and is a veteran of the U.S. Navy. Clark has served in numerous public, private, government and nonprofit capacities at various levels, from volunteer to chair. He was selected as the FBLA's Businessperson of the Year in North Carolina in 2019 and is also currently the chairman of the Outer Banks Community Foundation.

Married to a native Texan, he is the father of two young daughters and in his spare time enjoys time on the water and threadbare efforts to uncover the stories contained within old buildings.